Creative
CHICKEN

Food Editor: Rachel Blackmore
Subeditor: Ella Martin
Editorial Coordinator: Margaret Kelly
Editorial Assistant: Sheridan Packer
Recipe Development: Sheryle Eastwood, Carolyn
Fienberg, Joanne Glenn, Lucy Kelly, Anneka Mitchell,
Penelope Peel, Belinda Warn, Loukie Werle
Credits: Recipes pages 82, 90 by Louise Steel; pages 8,
73 by Lesley Mackley; pages 16, 17 by Lorna Rhodes ©
Merehurst Limited
Photography: Simon Butcher, Per Ericson, Paul Grater,
Ashley Mackevicius, Harm Mol, Yanto Noerianto,
Andrew Payne, Jon Stewart, Warren Webb
Styling: Wendy Berecry, Belinda Clayton, Carolyn
Fienberg, Anna Philips, Jacqui Hing, Michelle Gorry
Production Manager: Sheridan Carter
Layout: Lulu Dougherty
Cover Design: Frank Pithers
Finished Art: Gavin Murrell, Lulu Dougherty

Published by
J.B. Fairfax Press Pty Limited
80-82 McLachlan Avenue
Rushcutters Bay, NSW 2011, Australia
A.C.N. 003 738 430

JBFP 291R
Creative Chicken
Includes Index
ISBN 1 86343 122 5

Formatted by J.B. Fairfax Press Pty Limited
Printed by Toppan Printing Co, Singapore
PRINTED IN SINGAPORE

Creative CHICKEN

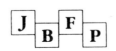

A J.B. Fairfax Press Publication

CONTENTS

SOUPS

Whether it's a clear consommé or a hearty chicken and vegetable, nothing beats homemade chicken soup. This selection of recipes shows you just how versatile chicken soup can be – there's something to suit all tastes.

Curried Chicken Soup

6

CURRIED CHICKEN SOUP

60 g/2 oz butter
2 onions, chopped
2 cloves garlic, crushed
2 large parsnips, chopped
2 stalks celery, chopped
3 tablespoons flour
1 tablespoon curry powder
6 cups/1.5 litres/2^{1}/$_{2}$ pt chicken stock
185 g/6 oz fresh or frozen green peas
500 g/1 lb cooked chicken, chopped
250 g/8 oz sour cream
3 tablespoons finely chopped parsley
2 tablespoons chopped fresh dill

1   Melt butter in a large saucepan and cook onions, garlic, parsnips and celery over a low heat for 5-6 minutes or until vegetables are just tender. Stir in flour and curry powder and cook for 1 minute longer.

2   Remove pan from heat and gradually blend in stock. Cook, stirring constantly, over a medium heat for 8-10 minutes or until soup boils and thickens. Reduce heat, stir in peas and chicken and cook for 10 minutes longer.

3   Remove pan from heat, whisk in sour cream, then stir in parsley and dill. Cook, stirring frequently, over a low heat for 3-4 minutes or until soup is heated. Serve immediately.

Serves 6

A hearty soup that only requires crusty bread to make it a complete meal.

CREAMY CHICKEN SOUP

15 g/^{1}/$_{2}$ oz butter
1 clove garlic, finely chopped
8 cups/2 litres/3^{1}/$_{2}$ pt chicken stock
1 kg/2 lb cooked chicken, finely chopped
2 teaspoons Worcestershire sauce
2 cups/500 mL/16 fl oz cream (double)
freshly ground black pepper
4 tablespoons chopped fresh parsley
4 tablespoons snipped fresh chives

1   Melt butter in a large saucepan and cook garlic over a low heat for 2-3 minutes. Add stock, bring to the boil, then reduce heat to simmering, stir in chicken and Worcestershire sauce, and cook for 2-3 minutes.

2   Stir in cream and season to taste with black pepper. Add parsley and chives and cook over a medium heat for 4-5 minutes or until soup is hot.

Serves 8

Cooked chicken is a quick and easy way to make chicken soup. But remember, do not cook the chicken for too long after adding to the soup or it will end up as unpalatable strings.

CHICKEN NOODLE SOUP

A homemade, well-seasoned, clear chicken broth filled with chicken, vegetables and noodles is a far cry from most of the packet soups you buy in food shops.

4 cups/1 litre/1³/₄ pt chicken stock
1 carrot, cut into matchsticks
1 leek, thinly sliced
125 g/4 oz cooked chicken, chopped
90 g/3 oz round egg noodles, broken into pieces
freshly ground black pepper
4 sprigs fresh coriander

1   Place stock in a large saucepan and bring to the boil. Add carrot and leek, cover, bring to simmering and simmer for 5 minutes or until carrot is tender.

2   Stir in chicken and noodles and cook for 5-10 minutes or until noodles are tender. Season to taste with black pepper. Serve garnished with coriander sprigs.

Serves 4

Chicken Noodle Soup

Chicken and Avocado Soup

CHICKEN AND AVOCADO SOUP

15 g/^{1}/2 oz butter
1 onion, finely chopped
1 large potato, diced
3 cups/750 mL/1^1/4 pt chicken stock
310 g/10 oz canned sweet
corn kernels, drained
375 g/12 oz cooked chicken, chopped
freshly ground black pepper
3 tablespoons cream or
evaporated skim milk
1 avocado, peeled, stoned and diced

1   Melt butter in a large saucepan and cook onion for 2-3 minutes or until soft. Stir in potato and stock, cover, bring to simmering and simmer for 10-15 minutes or until potato is tender.

2   Add corn, chicken and black pepper to taste and cook for 5-6 minutes or until soup is hot. Spoon soup into individual serving bowls. Swirl in cream or milk and top with avocado. Serve immediately.

Serves 4

Chicken and avocados seem to go together like bread and butter, and no more so than in this substantial soup. For a wonderful luncheon, serve the soup with crusty bread and follow with a mixed green salad.

Italian Chicken Soup

ITALIAN CHICKEN SOUP

12 cups/3 litres/5 pt chicken stock
4 boneless chicken breast fillets, skinned
1 teaspoon whole black peppercorns
4 bay leaves
1 sprig fresh rosemary
1 onion, chopped
1 red pepper, chopped
2 carrots, chopped
185 g/6 oz short pasta shapes,
such as macaroni
250 g/8 oz cabbage, shredded
2 tablespoons grated Parmesan cheese

1   Place stock in a large saucepan and bring to the boil. Add chicken breasts, peppercorns, bay leaves and rosemary. Reduce heat, cover and simmer for 20 minutes or until chicken is just cooked.

2   Using a slotted spoon, remove chicken from pan and set aside to drain. Strain stock and return liquid to a clean saucepan. Add onion, red pepper, carrots and pasta to stock, cover, then bring to simmering and simmer for 20 minutes or until pasta is cooked and vegetables are tender.

3   Slice chicken. Stir chicken and cabbage into soup and cook for 5 minutes longer. Just prior to serving, stir in Parmesan cheese.

Serves 6

This clear chicken broth made with fresh chicken and vegetables makes a nutritious and delicious light meal that any weight watcher will love.

CREAMY POTATO SOUP

90 g/3 oz butter
1 onion, chopped
2 cloves garlic, crushed
4 large potatoes, chopped
1 leek, chopped
3 cups/750 mL/1^1/4 pt chicken stock
^{1}/2 teaspoon ground nutmeg
1 cup/250 mL/8 fl oz cream (double)
freshly ground black pepper
2 tablespoons snipped fresh chives

CROUTONS
2 tablespoons vegetable oil
4 slices thick white bread, cut into
small strips

1   Melt butter in a large saucepan, add onion and garlic and cook, stirring, over a medium heat for 2 minutes. Add potatoes, leek, stock and nutmeg, bring to simmering and cook over a medium heat, stirring occasionally, for 20 minutes or until vegetables are tender.

2   Remove soup from heat and set aside to cool slightly. Place soup in batches in a food processor or blender and process until smooth.

3   Return soup to a clean saucepan, add cream and mix well to combine. Cook over a medium heat, stirring occasionally, for 10 minutes or until heated through. Season to taste with black pepper.

4   To make Croutons, heat oil in a frying pan over a medium heat, add bread strips and cook, turning frequently, for 2 minutes or until bread is golden. To serve, ladle soup into bowls, top with Croutons and sprinkle with chives.

Serves 4

A homemade chicken stock makes the difference to this creamy soup (see page 103 for making your own). Remember stock can be made in advance and frozen.

Creamy Potato Soup

CHILLI CHICKEN SOUP

100 g/3^1/$_2$ oz fresh egg noodles
2 tablespoons peanut oil
2 onions, chopped
2 cloves garlic, crushed
1 red chilli, finely sliced
1 teaspoon curry paste (vindaloo)
^{1}/$_4$ teaspoon ground turmeric
1 tablespoon finely chopped
fresh lemon grass or 1 tablespoon
finely grated lemon rind
4 cups/1 litre/1^3/$_4$ pt coconut milk
1^1/$_2$ cups/375 mL/12 fl oz chicken stock
375 g/12 oz cooked chicken, chopped
3 spinach leaves, finely shredded

1   Cook noodles in a large saucepan of boiling water for 3-4 minutes or until tender. Drain, then rinse noodles under cold running water. Drain again and place in individual bowls.

2   Heat oil in a large saucepan and cook onions for 2-3 minutes or until golden. Stir in garlic, chilli, curry paste, turmeric and lemon grass, and cook for 1 minute.

3   Combine coconut milk and chicken stock. Add coconut milk mixture, chicken and spinach to pan. Bring to simmering and simmer for 3-4 minutes. Spoon soup over noodles in bowls and serve immediately.

Serves 6

Coconut milk can be purchased canned, or as a long-life product in cartons, or as a powder to which you add water. These products have a short life once opened and should be used within a day or so.

Chilli Chicken Soup

You can make coconut milk using desiccated coconut and water. To make, place 500 g/1 lb desiccated coconut in a bowl and pour over 3 cups/750 mL/1^1/$_2$ pt of boiling water. Leave to stand for 30 minutes, then strain, squeezing the coconut to extract as much liquid as possible. This will make a thick coconut milk. The coconut can be used again to make a weaker coconut milk.

CHICKEN AND CORN SOUP

1 large potato, diced
1 large onion, sliced
6 cups/1.5 litres/2$^{1}/_{2}$ pt chicken stock
$^{1}/_{2}$ teaspoon chilli powder or
according to taste
250 g/8 oz cooked chicken, chopped
315 g/10 oz canned sweet corn
kernels, drained
2 tablespoons finely chopped
fresh parsley
freshly ground black pepper

1 Place potato, onion, stock and chilli powder in a large saucepan, bring to simmering and simmer for 20 minutes or until vegetables are tender.

2 Using a slotted spoon remove vegetables from soup, place in a food processor or blender and process until smooth.

3 Return vegetable purée to stock mixture and mix to combine. Add chicken and sweet corn to soup and cook, over a medium heat for 10 minutes or until heated through. Stir in parsley and season to taste with black pepper.

Serves 6

The puréed vegetables in this soup act as a thickening agent without adding kilojoules (calories).

COMBINATION NOODLE SOUP

2 teaspoons peanut oil
1 onion, finely chopped
1 red pepper, finely chopped
2 x 440 g/14 oz canned chicken
consommé
2 cups/ 500 mL/16 fl oz water
2 boneless chicken breast fillets, cooked
and thinly sliced
12 large uncooked prawns, shelled and
deveined
125 g/4 oz rice noodles, cooked
60 g/2 oz oyster mushrooms, sliced
60 g/2 oz canned bamboo shoots, sliced
4 lettuce leaves, shredded
1 tablespoon finely chopped
fresh coriander
freshly ground black pepper

1 Heat oil in a large saucepan, add onion and red pepper and cook, stirring frequently, for 5 minutes or until vegetables are tender.

2 Add consommé and water and bring to the boil. Reduce heat, add chicken, prawns, noodles, mushrooms and bamboo shoots and simmer for 5 minutes or until prawns turn pink and are just cooked.

3 Stir in lettuce, coriander and black pepper to taste and serve immediately.

Serves 6

A Chinese-style main meal soup that uses canned consommé as its base is a quick and tasty dish when time is short.

STARTERS

Chicken is especially popular for pre-dinner and cocktail nibbles. The recipes in this section lend themselves to being served as small portions for the first course of a formal dinner party or as finger food for a more informal occasion.

Mango Chicken Bites

MANGO CHICKEN BITES

1 teaspoon ground cardamom
2 teaspoons ground cumin
$^1/_2$ teaspoon chilli powder
1 teaspoon ground ginger
5 boneless chicken breast fillets,
cut into 2.5 cm/1 in pieces
2 tablespoons oil

MANGO SAUCE
1 cup/315 g/10 oz mango chutney
$^1/_4$ cup/60 mL/2 fl oz cream (double)
1 tablespoon curry powder

Serves 20 as an hors d'oeuvre

1 Place cardamom, cumin, chilli powder and ginger in a bowl and mix to combine. Add chicken and toss to coat with spice mixture. Cover and set aside to marinate at room temperature for 1 hour.

2 Heat oil in a frying pan and cook chicken, stirring, over a medium heat for 5 minutes or until cooked. Remove from pan and drain on absorbent kitchen paper.

3 To make sauce, place chutney, cream and curry powder in a food processor or blender and process to combine. Serve as a dipping sauce with chicken.

As a starter for a formal meal you might like to arrange the chicken pieces on a bed of mixed lettuce leaves with slices of fresh or canned mango. The Mango Sauce could be served in individual pots on the side of each plate.

ORIENTAL CHICKEN ROLLS

15g/$^1/_2$ oz Chinese dried mushrooms
boiling water
4 spring onions, chopped
60 g/2 oz fresh or frozen peas
freshly ground black pepper
2 boneless chicken breast fillets, cut into
12 strips lengthwise
12 sheets rice paper, cut in half
oil for deep frying

PLUM SAUCE
$^1/_2$ cup/125 mL/4 fl oz plum sauce
2 tablespoons water
2 tablespoons finely chopped cucumber

Makes 24 rolls

1 Place mushrooms in a bowl and cover with boiling water. Set aside to soak for 20 minutes or until mushrooms are tender. Drain, remove stalks and chop mushrooms.

2 Place mushrooms, spring onions and peas in a bowl and mix to combine. Season to taste with black pepper.

3 Place a chicken strip and 2 teaspoons mushroom mixture on a corner of each sheet of rice paper, tuck in edges and roll up. Seal, using a little water. Heat oil in a large saucepan and cook 3-4 rolls at a time for 2-3 minutes or until cooked – the rolls will not brown. Remove rolls from oil and drain on absorbent kitchen paper.

4 To make sauce, place plum sauce, water and cucumber in a bowl and mix to combine. Serve with hot rolls.

Chinese dried mushrooms are available from Oriental food shops. They are quite expensive, but keep indefinitely. As their flavour is very strong, only small quantities are used.

DUCK WITH CHERRY SAUCE

2 tablespoons seasoned flour
1 teaspoon five spice powder
750 g/1^1/$_2$ lb boneless duck breast fillets,
cut into 2.5 cm/1 in pieces
oil for deep frying

CHERRY SAUCE
1 tablespoon sugar
375 g/12 oz canned black cherries,
drained
^{1}/$_3$ cup/90 mL/3 fl oz red wine
^{1}/$_4$ teaspoon mixed spice

Serves 10 as an hors d'oeuvre

1 Place flour and five spice powder in a plastic food bag and shake to combine. Add duck and shake to coat all pieces.

2 Heat oil in a large saucepan and cook duck in batches for 3-4 minutes or until cooked and golden. Drain on absorbent kitchen paper.

3 To make sauce, place sugar, cherries, red wine and mixed spice in a saucepan. Bring to simmering and simmer, uncovered, for 15 minutes. Press cherry mixture through a sieve, return sieved sauce to a clean saucepan and heat gently for 3-4 minutes or until warm. Serve warm as a dipping sauce with hot duck.

Bite-sized pieces of spicy crisp duck are even more delicious when dipped in Cherry Sauce.

CHILLI CHICKEN WITH CURRY SAUCE

6 boneless chicken breast fillets, cut into
2.5 cm/1 in pieces
^{1}/$_3$ cup/90 mL/3 fl oz vegetable oil
2 teaspoons paprika
^{1}/$_2$ teaspoon chilli powder
oil for deep frying

CURRY SAUCE
1 tablespoon oil
1 onion, finely chopped
2 teaspoons mild curry powder
1 tablespoon flour
1^1/$_4$ cups/315 mL/10 fl oz milk
2 tablespoons mango chutney
freshly ground black pepper

Serves 10 as an hors d'oeuvre

1 Place chicken, vegetable oil, paprika and chilli powder in a bowl and mix to combine. Cover and set aside to marinate for 1 hour.

2 Heat oil in a large saucepan and cook chicken in batches for 3-4 minutes or until golden and cooked. Drain on absorbent kitchen paper.

3 To make sauce, heat oil in a saucepan and cook onion for 4-5 minutes or until soft. Stir in curry powder and cook for 2 minutes. Add flour and cook, stirring, for 1 minute longer. Gradually stir in milk and bring to the boil, stirring constantly, over a medium heat. Cook for 3-4 minutes or until sauce thickens, then reduce heat and simmer for 5 minutes longer. Stir in chutney and season to taste with black pepper. Serve warm as a dipping sauce with hot chicken.

Chilli-coated chicken pieces are delicious served with drinks or as a snack.

BACON AND MUSHROOM ROLLS

60 g/2 oz butter
1 onion, finely chopped
185 g/6 oz bacon, chopped
500 g/1 lb chicken livers, trimmed
and chopped
250 g/8 oz mushrooms, chopped
$^1/_2$ cup/125 mL/4 fl oz chicken stock
2 egg yolks, lightly beaten
$^1/_2$ teaspoon mixed dried herbs
freshly ground black pepper
4 sheets filo pastry
1 egg white
oil for deep frying

1   Melt butter in a large frying pan and
cook onion for 2-3 minutes or until soft.
Add bacon and cook for 3-4 minutes
longer. Stir in chicken livers and cook,
stirring, for 3 minutes or until livers
change colour. Add mushrooms and cook
for 3 minutes longer.

2   Stir in stock, bring to simmering and
simmer for 5 minutes or until almost all
stock has evaporated. Remove pan from
heat and set aside to cool for 10 minutes.

3   Mix egg yolks, mixed herbs and black
pepper to taste into chicken liver
mixture. Place chicken liver mixture in a
food processor and process to roughly
chop. Take care not to make a purée.

4   Cut pastry into twenty-four 15 cm/6 in
squares. Place 2 teaspoons of chicken
liver mixture on each pastry square, fold
in two edges and roll up like a spring roll.
Seal edges with a little egg white.

5   Heat oil in a large saucepan and cook
3-4 rolls at a time for 2-3 minutes or until
golden. Remove rolls from oil and drain
on absorbent kitchen paper.

Makes 24 rolls

*Duck with Cherry Sauce,
Bacon and Mushroom Rolls,
Chilli Chicken with Curry Sauce*

These crispy rolls filled with
chicken livers and
mushrooms can be prepared
in advance, leaving only the
final cooking until just prior to
serving. Serve with chilli
sauce and soy sauce as
dipping condiments.

SPRING ROLLS

12 spring roll or wonton wrappers, each
12.5 cm/5 in square
vegetable oil for deep frying

CHICKEN AND VEGETABLE
FILLING
125 g/4 oz chicken mince
30 g/1 oz bean sprouts
$^{1}/_{4}$ small cabbage, chopped
2 spring onions, chopped
1 tablespoon cornflour
1 tablespoon soy sauce
1 teaspoon sesame oil

1   To make filling, place chicken, bean sprouts, cabbage, spring onions, cornflour, soy sauce and sesame oil in a bowl and mix to combine.

2   Place a tablespoon of filling in the centre of each wrapper, fold one corner over filling, then tuck in the sides and roll up, sealing with water.

3   Heat vegetable oil in a large saucepan until a cube of bread browns in 50 seconds and cook a few Spring Rolls at a time for 3-4 minutes or until golden. Drain on absorbent kitchen paper and serve immediately.

Makes 12

CHICKEN AND LEEK ROLLS

12 spinach lasagne sheets
2 tablespoons grated fresh
Parmesan cheese

CHICKEN AND LEEK FILLING
2 teaspoons vegetable oil
3 leeks, finely sliced
3 boneless chicken breast fillets, cut
into thin strips
$^1/_2$ cup/125 mL/4 fl oz chicken stock
3 teaspoons cornflour blended with
2 tablespoons water
1 teaspoon French mustard
2 teaspoons chopped fresh basil
freshly ground black pepper

1   Cook lasagne sheets in boiling water
in a large saucepan until tender. Drain,
set aside and keep warm.

2   To make filling, heat oil in a large
frying pan and cook leeks and chicken,
stirring, for 4-5 minutes or until chicken
is brown. Stir in stock, cornflour mixture,
mustard and basil and cook, stirring, for 2
minutes longer. Season to taste with
black pepper.

3   Place spoonfuls of filling on lasagne
sheets, roll up, top with Parmesan cheese
and serve immediately.

Serves 6   *Chicken and Leek Rolls*

MAIN MEALS

Grilled, casseroled, fried, baked or roasted, chicken is a family favourite. Cooks love it because it is quick and easy to prepare, can be unadorned or dressed up and combines with many different flavours. These recipes for all kinds of birds are sure to give you many new ideas.

Feta Drumsticks

30 g/1 oz butter
1 clove garlic, crushed
1 bunch English spinach, finely
shredded
2 slices ham, finely chopped
125 g/4 oz feta cheese, broken
into small pieces
1 teaspoon ground coriander
3 teaspoons ground nutmeg
freshly ground black pepper
12 chicken drumsticks
2 tablespoons olive oil

1   Melt butter in a frying pan and cook garlic over a medium heat for 1 minute. Stir in half the spinach and cook for 3-4 minutes or until spinach is wilted. Remove cooked spinach from pan and set aside. Cook remaining spinach in the same way.

2   Place spinach, ham, feta cheese, coriander, 1 teaspoon nutmeg and black pepper to taste in a bowl and mix to combine. Ease skin carefully away from a drumstick to form a pocket. Place a spoonful of spinach mixture in pocket and pull skin over. Repeat with remaining spinach mixture and drumsticks. Brush drumsticks with oil, sprinkle with remaining nutmeg and place in a baking dish. Bake for 30 minutes or until drumsticks are cooked through.

Serves 6

Oven temperature
180°C, 350°F, Gas 4

These drumsticks are just as good cold or hot. Any leftovers are sure to be popular in packed lunches. If cooked the day before, they are perfect picnic fare.

Coconut Curry

1 tablespoon oil
4 boneless chicken breast fillets, skin
removed and halved
2 onions, cut into eighths
2 cloves garlic, chopped
2 tablespoons curry paste
1 1/2 cups/375 mL/12 fl oz water
3 potatoes, cut into cubes
3 carrots, sliced
2 stalks fresh lemon grass, bruised, or
1 teaspoon finely grated lemon rind
1 tablespoon cornflour
1/2 cup/125 mL/4 fl oz coconut milk

1   Heat oil in a large saucepan and cook chicken for 3-4 minutes or until brown on both sides. Remove chicken from pan and set aside. Add onions and garlic to pan and cook over a medium heat for 4-5 minutes or until onions are soft. Stir in curry paste and cook for 1 minute longer.

2   Return chicken to pan and stir in water, potatoes, carrots and lemon grass or lemon rind. Bring to the boil, then reduce heat, cover and simmer for 30 minutes or until chicken and vegetables are tender.

3   Whisk cornflour into coconut milk. Stir coconut milk mixture into chicken and cook, stirring, over a medium heat for 4-5 minutes or until curry boils and thickens. Cook for 3 minutes longer. Just prior to serving, remove lemon grass.

Feta Drumsticks

Serves 4

If commercially made coconut milk is unavailable, you can make it using desiccated coconut and water. To make coconut milk, place 500 g/1 lb desiccated coconut in a bowl and pour over 3 cups/ 750 mL/1 1/4 pt of boiling water. Leave to stand for 30 minutes, then strain, squeezing the coconut to extract as much liquid as possible. This will make a thick coconut milk. The coconut can be used again to make a weaker coconut milk.

RICE-FILLED CHICKEN

1 x 1.5 kg/3 lb chicken, cleaned
4 rashers bacon, chopped
4 spring onions, chopped
2 teaspoons curry powder
3/4 cup/170 g/5¹/2 oz long-grain
rice, cooked
1 cup/60 g/2 oz bread crumbs,
made from stale bread
1 tablespoon olive oil

MUSHROOM SAUCE
30 g/1 oz butter
1 onion, chopped
1 green pepper, chopped
125 g/4 oz mushrooms, sliced
440 g/14 oz canned tomatoes,
undrained and mashed
2 tablespoons tomato paste (purée)
3 tablespoons red wine
1 tablespoon sugar
¹/2 cup/125 mL/4 fl oz water
freshly ground black pepper

Serves 4

To test when a bird is
cooked, place a skewer into
the thickest part of the thigh
and when the skewer is
removed the juices should
run clear. If the juices are
tinged pink, return bird to the
oven and cook for 15
minutes longer, then test
again. On completion of
cooking, allow whole birds to
stand in a warm place for
10-20 minutes before carving.
This tenderises the meat by
allowing the juices to settle
into the flesh.

1   Using absorbent kitchen paper, pat
chicken dry inside and out. Cook bacon,
spring onions and curry powder in a frying
pan over a medium heat for 4-5 minutes
or until bacon is crisp. Remove pan from
heat and stir in rice and bread crumbs.

2   Fill cavity of chicken with rice
mixture and secure opening with metal or
bamboo skewers. Tuck wings under body
of chicken and tie legs together. Place
bird breast side up in a baking dish. Brush
with oil and bake, basting frequently with
pan juices, for 1¹/2 hours or until bird is
cooked.

3   To make sauce, melt butter in a
saucepan and cook onion, green pepper
and mushrooms for 2-3 minutes. Stir in
tomatoes, tomato paste (purée), wine,
sugar, water and black pepper to taste.
Cook, stirring constantly, over a medium
heat for 10-15 minutes or until sauce is
reduced by a quarter. Serve sauce with
chicken.

CHICKEN WITH CORN

1 tablespoon olive oil
2 onions, chopped
2 teaspoons ground cumin
4 chicken thighs
4 chicken drumsticks
1 cup/250 mL/8 fl oz dry white wine
1 cup/250 mL/8 fl oz chicken stock
1 cup/250 mL/8 fl oz cream (double)
315 g/10 oz canned sweet corn
kernels, drained

Serve this rich cumin-
flavoured chicken and corn
on a bed of boiled rice and
accompany with a green
vegetable such as beans,
asparagus or spinach.

1   Heat oil in a large frying pan and cook
onions and cumin over a medium heat for
4-5 minutes or until onions are soft. Add
chicken and cook for 8-10 minutes longer
or until brown on all sides. Transfer
onions and chicken to a casserole dish.

2   Drain fat from pan and stir in wine.
Bring to the boil, stirring and scraping
bits from base of pan. Boil for 4-5 minutes
or until reduced by half.

3   Stir stock, cream and corn into wine
and cook for 5 minutes longer. Pour wine
mixture over chicken, cover and bake for
45-60 minutes or until chicken is cooked.

Serves 4

Rice-filled Chicken

ALMOND CHICKEN ROLLS

4 boneless chicken breast fillets,
skin removed
vegetable oil for deep frying

BREAD CRUMB COATING
2 eggs
$^1/_3$ cup/90 mL/3 fl oz milk
$^1/_2$ cup/60 g/2 oz seasoned flour
2 cups/125 g/4 oz bread crumbs,
made from stale bread

HERB BUTTER
185 g/6 oz butter, softened
60 g/2 oz almonds, chopped
2 teaspoons French mustard
1 tablespoon chopped fresh parsley
1 tablespoon snipped fresh chives
freshly ground black pepper

Do not allow the oil to
become too hot when
cooking these rolls or the
coating will brown before the
chicken is cooked.

1   To make Herb Butter, place butter, almonds, mustard, parsley, chives and black pepper to taste in a bowl and mix to combine. Divide butter into four portions and shape into rolls 10 cm/4 in long. Wrap rolls in plastic food wrap and refrigerate until firm.

2   Place fillets between two sheets of plastic food wrap and pound, using a rolling pin, to flatten. Take care not to make holes in the fillets or the butter will run out during cooking.

3   Place a butter roll in the centre of each chicken fillet. Fold the shorter ends of the fillets into the centre, then roll up to fully encase the butter. Secure fillets with toothpicks.

4   To coat, place eggs and milk in a small bowl and beat to combine. Transfer to a shallow dish. Place flour and bread crumbs on separate plates. Coat chicken rolls with flour, then dip in egg mixture and roll in bread crumbs. Repeat egg and bread crumb steps. Place rolls on a plate, cover with plastic food wrap and refrigerate for 1 hour.

5   Heat oil in a large saucepan and cook chicken rolls for 5-8 minutes or until golden and cooked through.

Serves 4

Almond Chicken Rolls

CHICKEN BEAN BAKE

1 rasher bacon, chopped
1.5 kg/3 lb chicken pieces, skin removed
2 onions, chopped
1 clove garlic, crushed
$^1/_2$ cup/125 mL/4 fl oz chicken stock
$^1/_3$ cup/90 mL/3 fl oz white wine
1 teaspoon dried mixed herbs
1 teaspoon sugar
440 g/14 oz canned tomatoes, undrained and mashed
315 g/10 oz canned lima or butter beans, drained

1 Cook bacon in a frying pan, over a medium heat for 2-3 minutes or until crisp. Remove bacon from pan and drain on absorbent kitchen paper.

2 Cook chicken in frying pan for 5-8 minutes or until brown on all sides. Remove chicken from pan and place in a casserole.

3 Add onions and garlic to pan and cook for 2-3 minutes or until onion is soft. Scatter onion mixture and bacon over chicken pieces.

4 Stir stock, wine, herbs, sugar and tomatoes into pan and bring to the boil over a medium heat. Cook, stirring occasionally, until mixture reduces and thickens. Stir in beans and pour over chicken. Cover and bake for 45-60 minutes or until chicken is cooked.

Chicken Bean Bake   **Serves 6**

Oven temperature
200°C, 400°F, Gas 6

When cooking poultry pieces, remember that the breast – the white meat – cooks more quickly than the legs and thighs – the dark meat. Cooking the leg and thigh portions for 10 minutes before adding the breast portions will give you evenly cooked poultry pieces.

BLUEBERRY DUCK

2 tablespoons vegetable oil
4 duck breasts, with skin
3 tablespoons balsamic or
red wine vinegar
$^1/_4$ teaspoon ground cinnamon
4 tablespoons fresh blueberries
freshly ground black pepper
ZUCCHINI (COURGETTE)
FLOWERS
$^3/_4$ cup/90 g/3 oz flour
1 cup/250 mL/8 fl oz water
vegetable oil for deep frying
12 zucchini (courgette) flowers

Blueberries are used in this recipe, but any other berry fruit can be used instead.

In Italy, zucchini (courgette) flowers are used in many ways. They can be dipped in batter and fried, or stuffed and then fried or used in risotto. If zucchini (courgette) flowers are unavailable, do not be put off making this dish – the duck is just as good served with a green vegetable such as asparagus, beans or zucchini (courgettes).

1 Heat oil in a large frying pan and cook duck, skin side down, over a low heat for 4-5 minutes or until skin is golden. Turn and cook other side for 3-4 minutes.

2 Add vinegar, cinnamon, blueberries and black pepper to taste. Cover and cook over a low heat for 15 minutes or until duck is tender.

3 To prepare flowers, gradually sift flour into water and mix with a fork until batter is smooth. If necessary, add more water. Pour 2.5 cm/1 in oil into a frying pan and heat until very hot. Dip flowers into batter and cook a few at a time in oil until golden.

4 To serve, arrange duck and flowers on a serving plate and spoon blueberry sauce over duck.

Serves 4

CHICKEN MARSALA

4 boneless chicken breast fillets,
pounded
3 tablespoons seasoned flour
30 g/1 oz butter
2 tablespoons olive oil
$^3/_4$ cup/185 mL/6 fl oz dry Marsala
or sherry
$^1/_3$ cup/90 mL/3 fl oz chicken stock
30 g/1 oz butter, softened
freshly ground black pepper

To pound chicken breast fillets, place fillets between two sheets of plastic food wrap and pound, using a rolling pin, to flatten. Take care not to make holes in the fillets. This method of pounding also prevents the fillets from sticking to the pounding utensil.

1 Coat chicken in flour and shake off excess. Heat butter and oil in a large frying pan, until butter is foaming. Add chicken and cook for 3 minutes each side.

2 Stir in Marsala or sherry, bring to the boil, reduce heat and simmer for 15 minutes or until chicken is cooked. Remove chicken and set aside to keep warm. Add stock, bring to the boil and boil for 2 minutes. Whisk in softened butter and season to taste with black pepper. To serve, spoon sauce over chicken.

Serves 4

*Quail with Olive Rice, Blueberry Duck,
Chicken Marsala*

QUAIL WITH OLIVE RICE

1 tablespoon olive oil
30 g/1 oz butter
2 onions, chopped
2 cloves garlic, crushed
8 quails
5 fresh sage leaves
3 teaspoons chopped fresh rosemary or
1 teaspoon dried rosemary
freshly ground black pepper
$1^1/4$ cups/315 mL/10 fl oz dry sherry

OLIVE RICE
375 g/12 oz rice, cooked
60 g/2 oz butter, chopped
6 slices mortadella, chopped
90 g/3 oz pitted black olives, chopped
3 tablespoons grated fresh
Parmesan cheese
3 tablespoons chopped fresh basil

1   Heat oil and butter in a frying pan and cook onions and garlic over a low heat for 3 minutes or until onions are soft.

2   Add quails to pan and cook over a high heat until brown on all sides. Add sage, rosemary and black pepper to taste.

3   Stir in sherry, bring to the boil, then reduce heat and simmer for 20 minutes or until quails are cooked.

4   To prepare rice, place rice, butter, mortadella and olives in a saucepan and cook, stirring, over a low heat for 4-5 minutes until butter is melted and mixture is hot. Mix in Parmesan cheese and basil. To serve, divide rice between four serving plates, top with quails and spoon a little of the pan juices over.

Serves 4

How do you eat quail? In your fingers.
Just as eating asparagus in your fingers is considered permissible, the same goes for quail. In fact, eating quail any other way is very difficult and you leave behind much of the delicious meat.

ORIENTAL STIR-FRY

2 tablespoons vegetable oil
2 onions, cut into eighths
1 clove garlic, crushed
1 teaspoon grated fresh ginger
8 boneless chicken breast fillets,
cut into strips
$1/4$ teaspoon ground cumin
$1/4$ teaspoon ground coriander
3 tablespoons oyster sauce
1 teaspoon sesame oil
125 g/4 oz broccoli, cut into florets
125 g/4 oz snow peas (mangetout),
trimmed
1 tablespoon sesame seeds

1   Heat oil in a frying pan or wok and stir-fry onions, garlic and ginger for 2-3 minutes or until onion is soft. Remove from pan and set aside.

2   Add chicken to pan and stir-fry for 3-4 minutes or until chicken changes colour. Place cumin, coriander, oyster sauce and sesame oil in a small bowl, mix to combine, then stir into pan. Return onion mixture to pan, add broccoli and snow peas (mangetout) and stir-fry for 3-4 minutes or until broccoli and snow peas (mangetout) are tender. Sprinkle with sesame seeds and serve immediately.

Serves 4

A quick and easy Asian-style dish with a medley of flavours that is sure to be popular. Serve with boiled rice or noodles for a complete meal.

HERB CHUTNEY CHICKEN

1 x 1.5 kg/3 lb chicken
60 g/2 oz butter, melted
2 cloves garlic, crushed

CHUTNEY STUFFING
2 tablespoons chopped fresh mixed
herbs such as parsley, chives, rosemary,
thyme and oregano
125 g/4 oz grated fresh Parmesan cheese
2 tablespoons fruit chutney
1 egg, lightly beaten
1 cup/60 g/2 oz dried bread crumbs
90 g/3 oz butter, melted

Herb Chutney Chicken

1   To make stuffing, place herbs, Parmesan cheese, chutney, egg, bread crumbs and butter in a bowl and mix to combine. Fill cavity of chicken with stuffing and secure opening with metal or bamboo skewers.

2   Tuck wings under body of chicken and tie legs together. Place bird breast side up in a baking dish. Combine butter and garlic, brush over chicken and bake, turning several times, for 1-1^1/$_2$ hours or until bird is cooked.

Serves 4

Oven temperature
180°C, 350°F, Gas 4

When making stuffing, try doubling the quantity and cooking the remainder in a dish to serve as extra stuffing with the bird. Or use to fill vegetables such as tomatoes and red and green peppers. These vegetables will take 20-30 minutes to cook and can be baked with the chicken.

PIMENTO CHICKEN PIE

Oven temperature
180°C, 350°F, Gas 4

A chicken pie with a difference. The Polenta Pastry has a deliciously different texture and the filling is like no other you have tasted. For a complete meal, serve with a salad of mixed lettuces, tomatoes and olives tossed in a light vinaigrette dressing.

POLENTA PASTRY
1^1/2 cups/185 g/12 oz flour
^{1}/3 cup/60 g/2 oz polenta (corn meal)
155 g/5 oz butter, cut into pieces
1 egg, lightly beaten
^{1}/2 cup/125 mL/4 fl oz water

CHICKEN PIMENTO FILLING
1 tablespoon olive oil
500 g/1 lb frozen spinach, thawed
2 cloves garlic, crushed
30 g/1 oz pine nuts
5 slices prosciutto or ham, chopped
3 boneless chicken breast fillets, poached and chopped
2 pieces canned pimento or ^{1}/2 red pepper, cut into strips
3 eggs, lightly beaten
1 cup/250 mL/8 fl oz cream (double)
freshly ground black pepper

1   To make pastry, place flour, polenta (corn meal) and butter in a food processor and process until mixture resembles fine bread crumbs. With machine running, add egg, then water a tablespoon at a time until mixture forms a ball. Turn dough onto a lightly floured surface and knead lightly. Wrap in plastic food wrap and refrigerate for 30 minutes.

2   To make filling, heat oil in a large frying pan and cook spinach, garlic, pine nuts and prosciutto or ham over a medium heat for 4-5 minutes or until pine nuts are golden. Transfer spinach mixture to a bowl and set aside to cool completely. Add chicken, pimento or red pepper, eggs and cream, and mix to combine.

3   Roll out two-thirds of polenta dough on a lightly floured surface and line the base and sides of a lightly greased, deep 23 cm/9 in pie dish. Trim edges using a sharp knife. Spoon filling into pie dish. On a lightly floured surface, roll out remaining pastry large enough to cover pie. Brush edge of pastry with water and cover with pastry top. Press edges together to seal, then trim and make a decorative edge using fingertips. Make two slits in top of pie to allow steam to escape. Bake for 45 minutes or until pastry is golden.

Serves 8

Pimento Chicken Pie

CHICKEN ROLL CASSEROLE

6 boneless chicken breast fillets,
skin removed
3 rashers bacon
1 tablespoon chopped fresh parsley
60 g/2 oz butter
2 onions, chopped
2 carrots, grated
8 spinach leaves
freshly ground black pepper
3 potatoes, cooked
$^1/_2$ cup/125 mL/4 fl oz water

1 Place fillets between two sheets of plastic food wrap and pound, using a rolling pin, to flatten. Remove rind from bacon and cut each rasher in half. Place a piece of bacon on each chicken fillet and sprinkle with parsley. Fold the shorter ends of the fillets into the centre, then roll up and secure fillets with toothpicks.

2 Melt half the butter in a large frying pan and cook chicken rolls for 8-10 minutes or until brown on all sides. Remove rolls from pan and set aside.

3 Melt remaining butter in frying pan and cook onions and carrots, stirring, for 5 minutes or until onions are soft. Add spinach and cook, stirring, for 2-3 minutes longer or until spinach is wilted. Season to taste with black pepper.

4 Cut potatoes into thick slices and place in the base of a casserole dish. Top with vegetable mixture, then chicken rolls. Pour water over, cover and bake for 35-40 minutes or until chicken rolls are cooked.

Serves 6

Oven temperature
180°C, 350°F, Gas 4

Chicken rolls filled with bacon and parsley make a complete meal when teamed with vegetables and cooked in a casserole. Serve with crusty bread rolls or garlic bread.

Chicken Roll Casserole

Honeyed Roast Quail

HONEYED ROAST QUAIL

Oven temperature
180°C, 350°F, Gas 4

Native to the Middle East, the quail is the smallest game bird and is related to the pheasant. It is now reared on farms and considered a gourmet item. Due to the small size of the bird, two are usually considered to be a serving.

4 quails

SOY HONEY GLAZE
1 tablespoon sesame oil
$^1/4$ cup/60 mL/2 fl oz soy sauce
$^1/4$ cup/90 g/3 oz honey
2 tablespoons lemon juice
1 tablespoon sesame seeds

1   To make glaze, place oil, soy sauce, honey, lemon juice and sesame seeds in a small saucepan and cook, stirring, over a medium heat for 10 minutes.

2   Tuck wings under body of each quail and tie legs together. Place breast side up in a baking dish and brush with glaze. Bake, basting several times, for 25 minutes or until birds are cooked.

Serves 2

CHICKEN TERRINE

1 x 1.5 kg/3 lb chicken
8 cups/2 litres/3^1/$_2$ pt water
2 carrots, chopped
2 onions, quartered
60 g/2 oz chopped fresh parsley
1 tablespoon black peppercorns
4 bay leaves
1 tablespoon gelatine
^{1}/$_4$ cup/60 mL/2 fl oz boiling water
2 stalks celery, finely chopped
2 spring onions, finely chopped
30 g/1 oz basil leaves, chopped
250 g/8 oz ham slices, chopped

1   Place chicken, water, carrots, onions, parsley, peppercorns and bay leaves in a large saucepan and bring to the boil. Reduce heat and simmer for 2 hours.

2   Remove chicken from cooking liquid and set aside to cool completely. Strain stock into a bowl and discard vegetables.

3   Strip flesh from chicken, discarding skin and bones. Place chicken flesh in a food processor and process to roughly chop. Take care not to process to a paste.

4   Place strained stock in a clean saucepan, bring to the boil, then reduce heat and simmer, uncovered, until stock is reduced to 3 cups/750 mL/1^1/$_4$ pt. Dissolve gelatine in boiling water then stir into hot stock. Set aside to cool slightly.

5   Place celery, spring onions and basil in a bowl, and mix to combine. Place ham in the base of a loaf tin lined with plastic food wrap, then top with celery mixture and finally with chicken. Pour over stock mixture and press down to evenly distribute stock and to immerse chicken. Cover and refrigerate until set. To serve, turn terrine onto a plate and slice.

Serves 8

Ideal for a garden party or even to take on a picnic, this terrine takes time to prepare, but the delicious flavour makes it worthwhile. One shortcut would be to use a barbecued chicken and commercial chicken stock.

Chicken Terrine

AVOCADO STRUDEL

Oven temperature
180°C, 350°F, Gas 4

This recipe is also delicious made with tuna or salmon in place of the chicken. For a lower kilojoule (calorie) version, ricotta cheese can be used instead of cream cheese.

10 sheets filo pastry
4 tablespoons vegetable oil
2 tablespoons sesame seeds

CHICKEN AVOCADO FILLING
1 tablespoon oil
1 small onion, chopped
2 teaspoons curry powder
200 g/6$^{1}/_{2}$ oz cream cheese, softened
2 boneless chicken breast fillets,
cooked and cut into strips
$^{1}/_{2}$ red pepper, sliced
8 button mushrooms, sliced
1 avocado, stoned, peeled and sliced
freshly ground black pepper

1   To make filling, heat oil in a frying pan and cook onion and curry powder for 4-5 minutes or until onion is soft. Transfer onion mixture to a bowl, add cream cheese, chicken, red pepper, mushrooms, avocado and black pepper to taste. Mix well to combine.

2   Layer filo pastry sheets on top of each other, brushing between layers with oil. Top pastry with chicken mixture and roll up tightly, tucking ends under. Place on a baking tray, brush with oil, sprinkle with sesame seeds and bake for 30 minutes or until golden.

Avocado Strudel

Serves 6

CHICKEN BIRYANI

90 g/3 oz ghee or butter
3 onions, sliced
1.5 kg/3 lb chicken pieces
2 teaspoons grated fresh ginger
3 cloves garlic, crushed
$^1/_2$ teaspoon ground cumin
$^1/_2$ teaspoon ground cinnamon
$^1/_4$ teaspoon ground cloves
$^1/_4$ teaspoon ground cardamom
$^1/_4$ teaspoon ground nutmeg
$^1/_2$ teaspoon flour
1 cup/250 mL/8 fl oz chicken stock
$^1/_2$ cup/100 g/3$^1/_2$ oz natural yogurt
$^1/_2$ cup/125 mL/4 fl oz cream (double)
60 g/2 oz roasted cashew nuts, chopped

RICE PILAU
60 g/2 oz ghee
$^1/_2$ teaspoon ground saffron
$^1/_2$ teaspoon ground cardamom
1 teaspoon salt
1 cup/220 g/7 oz basmati rice,
well-washed
4 cups/1 litre/1$^3/_4$ pt chicken stock
2 tablespoons sultanas

1   Heat ghee or butter in a large frying pan and cook onions, stirring, over a medium heat for 5 minutes or until golden. Remove from pan and set aside.

Add chicken to pan and cook for 3-4 minutes each side or until golden. Remove from pan and set aside.

2   Add ginger, garlic, cumin, cinnamon, cloves, cardamom, nutmeg and flour to pan and cook, stirring, for 1-2 minutes. Add stock, yogurt and cream, stirring to lift sediment from base of pan. Return chicken and half the onion mixture to pan, cover and simmer for 15-20 minutes or until chicken is just cooked. Remove pan from heat and stand, covered, for 15 minutes.

3   To make pilau, melt ghee or butter in a large saucepan and cook saffron, cardamom, salt and rice, stirring constantly, for 1-2 minutes. Add stock and bring to the boil. Stir in sultanas, reduce heat and simmer for 10-15 minutes or until most of the stock is absorbed and rice is cooked. Cover and set aside to stand for 10 minutes.

4   Place rice on a large ovenproof serving platter, top with chicken pieces and spoon sauce over. Sprinkle with remaining onions and cashew nuts, cover and bake for 20 minutes.

Serves 4

Oven temperature
180°C, 350°F, Gas 4

The Great Moguls (Muslim emperors of India between 1526 and 1857) served biryani at lavish feasts on plates so large that two people were required to carry them.

Chicken Biryani

CHICKEN POT PIE

Oven temperature
200°C, 400°F, Gas 6

A delicious herb topping is an imaginative alternative to potatoes in this cobbler-style recipe. Serve with a green vegetable, such as beans, spinach or cabbage, for a complete meal.

60 g/2 oz butter
1 large onion, chopped
4 boneless chicken breast fillets,
cut into 2 cm/³/4 in cubes
2 potatoes, cut into 1 cm/¹/2 in cubes
2 large carrots, cut into
1 cm/¹/2 in cubes
¹/4 cup/30 g/1 oz flour
1 cup/250 mL/8 fl oz dry white wine
3 cups/750 mL/1¹/4 pt chicken stock
1 cup/250 mL/8 fl oz cream (double)
2 tablespoons tomato paste (purée)

HERBED SCONE TOPPING
2 cups/250 g/8 oz self-raising
flour, sifted
1 teaspoon dried mixed herbs
30 g/1 oz grated fresh Parmesan cheese
30 g/1 oz butter, chopped
1 cup/250 mL/8 fl oz milk

1 Melt butter in a large frying pan and cook onion, stirring, over a medium heat for 3-4 minutes or until onion is soft. Add chicken and cook, stirring, for 3 minutes longer.

2 Add potatoes and carrots and cook, stirring, for 8-10 minutes. Stir in flour, then wine, stock, cream and tomato paste (purée), and bring to simmering. Simmer for 10 minutes then transfer mixture to a casserole dish.

3 To make topping, place flour, herbs, Parmesan cheese and butter in a food processor and process to combine. With machine running, add milk and process to form a sticky dough. Turn dough onto a lightly floured surface and knead until smooth. Press dough out to 2 cm/³/4 in thick and, using a scone cutter, cut out rounds and place on top of casserole.

4 Bake for 20-25 minutes or until topping is cooked and golden, and casserole is hot.

Serves 4

Chicken Pot Pie

Herbed Poussins

HERBED POUSSINS

4 poussins
4 sprigs fresh thyme
4 rashers bacon, rind removed

HERB BUTTER MARINADE
1 tablespoon dried mixed herbs
90 g/3 oz butter, melted
3 tablespoons vegetable oil

Serves 4

1   To make marinade, place herbs, butter and oil in a small bowl and mix to combine.

2   Place a sprig of thyme in cavity of each poussin. Tuck wings under poussins and tie legs together. Wrap a bacon rasher around each bird and secure with a toothpick. Place birds breast side up in a baking dish, brush with marinade and bake, basting frequently with marinade, for 30-35 minutes or until cooked.

Oven temperature
180°C, 350°F, Gas 4

Delicious served with a tossed salad of mixed lettuce and fresh herbs and crusty wholemeal rolls.

37

REDCURRANT DUCK

2 tablespoons olive oil
8 duck breasts, with skin
$^1/_4$ cup/60 mL/2 fl oz fresh lime
or lemon juice
2 tablespoons honey
$^1/_2$ cup/170 g/5$^1/_2$ oz redcurrant jelly
125 g/4 oz fresh or frozen redcurrants

Pan-cooked duck breasts with a redcurrant sauce make an elegant main course. Serve with asparagus, a sauté of leek strips and new potatoes.

1 Heat oil in a large frying pan and cook duck breasts for 7-8 minutes each side or until golden and cooked to your liking. Remove from pan, set aside and keep warm.

2 Drain fat from pan and add lime or lemon juice, honey and redcurrant jelly. Bring to the boil over a medium heat, stirring to lift sediment from base of pan. Reduce heat and simmer for 3-4 minutes or until mixture reduces and thickens slightly. Stir in redcurrants and cook, stirring, for 1 minute longer. Serve sauce with duck.

Serves 4

CHICKPEA RAGOUT

$^1/_4$ cup/60 mL/2 fl oz olive oil
1 onion, chopped
1 teaspoon ground turmeric
1 x 1.5 kg/3 lb chicken, cut
into 6 pieces
220 g/7 oz chickpeas, soaked
overnight, drained
2 cups/500 mL/16 fl oz chicken stock
$^1/_4$ cup/60 mL/2 fl oz fresh lemon juice
3 cloves garlic, crushed
30 g/1 oz blanched almonds, toasted
1 tablespoon chopped fresh parsley

Chickpeas take 45-60 minutes to cook. The cooking time can vary depending on the quality and age of the chickpeas and their place of origin. This recipe could be made using canned chickpeas. If using canned chickpeas, heat oil in a large frying pan and cook onion, turmeric, chicken and garlic, stirring, for 4-5 minutes. Transfer chicken mixture to a saucepan and stir in 2 tablespoons lemon juice, 1 cup/250 mL/8 fl oz stock (the remaining lemon juice and stock will not be used in this version of the recipe) and chickpeas. Bring to simmering and simmer for 15-20 minutes or until hot. Just prior to serving, sprinkle with almonds and parsley.

1 Heat oil in a large frying pan and cook onion and turmeric, stirring, over a medium heat for 3 minutes or until onion is soft. Add chicken pieces and cook for 4 minutes each side or until golden. Remove chicken pieces from pan and set aside.

2 Add chickpeas, stock, lemon juice and garlic to pan, bring to the boil, then reduce heat and simmer for 40 minutes. Return chicken to pan and simmer for 20 minutes longer or until chicken and chickpeas are tender. Just prior to serving, sprinkle with almonds and parsley.

Serves 4

Redcurrant Duck,
Chickpea Ragout

SALADS

Served with crusty bread and a salad of mixed lettuces, chicken salads are the most delicious of summer meals. In this chapter you will find recipes not only for chicken salads but also for a marvellous Creamy Roast Duck Salad and an elegant Spinach and Chicken Liver Salad.

Fruity Smoked Chicken Salad

Fruity Smoked Chicken Salad

2 ripe pears, cored and halved vertically
1 x 1.5 kg/3 lb smoked chicken, skin
removed, cut into strips

WATERCRESS DRESSING
30 g/1 oz butter
1 small bunch watercress
4 spring onions, chopped
1 clove garlic, crushed
2 teaspoons tarragon vinegar
1 tablespoon dry white wine
1 cup/250 mL/8 fl oz cream (double)

Serves 4 as a starter or light meal

1 To make dressing, melt butter in a
saucepan, stir in watercress, spring onions,
garlic, vinegar and white wine and bring
to simmering over a medium heat.
Simmer for 5 minutes, then stir in cream
and simmer, uncovered, for 10 minutes
longer or until dressing reduces and
thickens. Remove from heat and set aside
to cool for 10 minutes. Place dressing in a
food processor or blender and process
until smooth. Set aside to cool
completely.

2 Cut each pear half into slices vertically
from the base without cutting through
top. Fan pear and arrange attractively on
plate with chicken. Spoon dressing over
chicken and serve immediately.

Smoked chicken is one of the
more recent food products
and is available from some
supermarkets and
delicatessens. It has been
cured and smoked and has
a pale pink flesh with a
delicate flavour.

Tomato and Chicken Salad

1 loaf unsliced wholegrain bread
3 tablespoons olive oil
4 rashers bacon, cut into strips
1 cooked chicken, skin removed and
flesh cut into bite-sized pieces
250 g/8 oz cherry tomatoes,
cut into quarters
2 spring onions, finely chopped
freshly ground black pepper
6 fresh basil sprigs

BASIL MAYONNAISE
1 clove garlic, crushed
60 g/2 oz fresh basil leaves
1 cup/250 g/8 oz mayonnaise

1 Remove crusts from bread and cut
into 2.5 cm/1 in cubes. Place in a bowl
and sprinkle with olive oil. Toss to coat
bread cubes evenly with oil. Arrange
bread cubes in a single layer on a baking

tray and bake for 10-15 minutes or until
golden and toasted. Set aside to cool.

2 Cook bacon in a frying pan for 4-5
minutes or until crisp. Remove bacon
from pan, drain on absorbent kitchen
paper and set aside to cool.

3 To make mayonnaise, place garlic,
basil leaves and 1 tablespoon mayonnaise
in a food processor or blender and process
to purée. Add remaining mayonnaise and
process to combine.

4 Place chicken, tomatoes, spring
onions, black pepper to taste and half the
bacon in a large salad bowl. Top with
mayonnaise and toss to coat all
ingredients. Divide salad between six
plates, place croutons around edge of each
plate, sprinkle with remaining bacon and
garnish with basil sprigs.

Oven temperature
180°C, 350°F, Gas 4

This easy-to-prepare chicken
salad is a main course meal
in itself that needs no other
accompaniment.

Serves 6 as a main meal

WARM ORIENTAL CHICKEN SALAD

The best way to cook a chicken for a chicken salad is to place it breast side down in a saucepan. Pour over enough cold water just to cover the bird. Cut 1 onion into thick slices and add to pan with 4 peppercorns and several sprigs of parsley. Bring to the boil over a medium heat, then reduce heat, cover and simmer for 45 minutes or until chicken is cooked. Transfer chicken and cooking liquid to a large bowl. Ensure that chicken is breast side down in the bowl so that the breast flesh remains moist. Cover and refrigerate until cold.

220 g/7 oz cellophane or
transparent noodles
boiling water
1 cooked chicken, skin removed
and flesh shredded
1 carrot, grated
3 tablespoons chopped fresh coriander
1 cucumber, chopped
30 g/1 oz peanuts, chopped

PEANUT DRESSING
2 cloves garlic, crushed
1/4 cup/60 mL/2 fl oz soy sauce
1/4 cup/60 mL/2 fl oz fresh lemon juice
1 tablespoon peanut butter
1/3 cup/90 mL/3 fl oz vegetable oil
1 tablespoon brown sugar

1   Place noodles in a large heatproof bowl, pour over boiling water to cover and set aside to stand for 10 minutes. Drain.

2   Place chicken, carrot, coriander and cucumber in a bowl and mix to combine.

3   To make dressing, place garlic, soy sauce, lemon juice, peanut butter, oil and sugar in a small saucepan and bring to the boil, stirring, over a medium heat. Cook, stirring, for 3 minutes. Pour dressing over chicken and toss to combine.

4   Divide noodles between four plates, top with chicken mixture and sprinkle with peanuts. Serve immediately.

Serves 4 as a main meal

CHICKEN AND ORANGE SALAD

1 cooked chicken, skin removed and flesh cut into bite-sized pieces
2 stalks celery, sliced
220 g/7 oz canned water chestnuts, drained and halved
1 orange, segmented
1 red onion, chopped

TARRAGON DRESSING
1 tablespoon chopped fresh parsley
$^1/_3$ cup/90 mL/3 fl oz safflower oil
1 clove garlic, crushed
$^1/_4$ cup/60 mL/2 fl oz tarragon vinegar

1   Place chicken, celery, water chestnuts, orange segments and onion in a salad bowl. Toss gently to combine.

2   To make dressing, place parsley, oil, garlic and vinegar in a screwtop jar, and shake well to combine. Pour over salad and toss gently.

Serves 4

Chunks of tender chicken, pieces of crunchy celery and water chestnuts team with fresh-tasting orange segments to make the perfect summer lunch.

Chicken and Orange Salad

SPINACH AND CHICKEN LIVER SALAD

6 slices white bread, crusts removed
60 g/2 oz butter
250 g/8 oz chicken livers, trimmed
3 tablespoons brandy
1 tablespoon dried mixed herbs
250 g/8 oz spinach, stalks
removed and discarded
$^1/_4$ cup/60 mL/2 fl oz dry white wine
1 tablespoon olive oil
1 red pepper, finely chopped

1   Using biscuit cutters, cut bread into decorative shapes. Melt half the butter in a frying pan over a medium heat until bubbling. Add bread and cook for 1-2 minutes each side or until golden. Remove croutons from pan and drain on absorbent kitchen paper.

2   Melt remaining butter in frying pan and cook chicken livers, stirring constantly, for 2-3 minutes. Add brandy and herbs and cook for 3 minutes longer.

3   Arrange spinach on a large platter or in a salad bowl. Using a slotted spoon remove chicken livers from pan, slice and scatter over spinach. Add wine to pan and cook over a medium heat for 2 minutes, strain mixture into small bowl and discard any sediment. Add oil to strained mixture and mix to combine. Spoon dressing over salad, then top with croutons and red pepper.

Warm chicken livers, pretty-shaped croutons and spinach combine to make an attractive starter.

Spinach and Chicken Liver Salad

Serves 4 as a starter or light meal

CREAMY ROAST DUCK SALAD

1 x 2 kg/4 lb duck
freshly ground black pepper
2 tablespoons chopped fresh parsley

CREAMY ONION DRESSING
2 red onions, cut into wedges
2 tablespoons vegetable oil
$^3/_4$ cup/185 mL/6 fl oz chicken stock
$^1/_2$ cup/125 mL/4 fl oz dry white wine
$^3/_4$ cup/185 g/6 oz sour cream

1 Season duck with black pepper. Tuck wings under body of duck and tie legs together. Place bird breast side up on a wire rack set in a baking dish and bake for 1 hour or until duck is cooked. Remove from pan and set aside to cool completely.

2 To make dressing, separate onion wedges. Heat oil in a frying pan and cook onions for 5 minutes or until soft. Stir in stock and cook for 8 minutes. Add wine, bring to the boil, then reduce heat and simmer, stirring, to lift sediment from base of pan for 5 minutes. Remove pan from heat, transfer contents to a bowl and set aside to cool to room temperature. Place sour cream in a bowl, add stock mixture and mix well to combine.

3 Remove skin from duck and discard. Strip flesh from duck, cut into bite-sized pieces and place in a bowl. Add dressing and toss to combine. Just prior to serving, sprinkle with parsley. Serve salad at room temperature or chilled.

Serves 4 as a light meal

Oven temperature
180°C, 350°F, Gas 4

Serve this delicious duck salad with boiled new potatoes or a plain rice dish and cold asparagus spears.

Creamy Roast Duck Salad

CRUNCHY CHICKEN SALAD

1 tablespoon vegetable oil
4 boneless chicken breast fillets
6 stalks celery, cut into strips
6 spring onions, chopped
$^{1}/_{2}$ cup/60 g/2 oz roughly chopped
pecans

SOUR CREAM DRESSING
1 cup/250 g/8 oz sour cream
$^{1}/_{2}$ cup/125 mL/4 fl oz mayonnaise
freshly ground black pepper

1   To make dressing, place sour cream, mayonnaise and black pepper to taste in a bowl and whisk to combine.

2   Heat oil in a large frying pan, add chicken and cook over a medium-high heat for 4-5 minutes each side or until cooked through. Remove chicken from pan and set aside to cool. Cut cold chicken into strips.

3   Place chicken and dressing in a salad bowl and toss to coat. Add celery, spring onions and pecans to chicken mixture and toss well to combine. Cover and refrigerate for 1 hour before serving.

Serves 4

For a lower kilojoule (calorie) dressing replace the sour cream with natural yogurt and the mayonnaise with a low-oil mayonnaise.

Left: Crunchy Chicken Salad
Below: Chicken and Walnut Salad

CHICKEN AND WALNUT SALAD

¹/₂ cup/60 g/2 oz chopped walnuts
1 x 1.5 kg/3 lb smoked chicken, skin
removed and flesh cut into strips
2 green apples

WALNUT VINAIGRETTE
¹/₄ cup/60 mL/2 fl oz white wine vinegar
¹/₄ cup/60 mL/2 fl oz walnut oil
1 tablespoon finely chopped fresh
coriander
freshly ground black pepper

1   Place walnuts in a shallow ovenproof
dish and bake, stirring occasionally, for 15
minutes or until nuts are toasted. Remove
from oven and set aside to cool.

2   To make vinaigrette, place vinegar,
oil, coriander and black pepper to taste in
a screwtop jar and shake well to combine.

3   Cut apples into quarters, remove core
then cut each quarter into three slices.

4   Place chicken, apples and walnuts in a
salad bowl. Spoon vinaigrette over
chicken mixture and toss well to combine.
Serve immediately.

Serves 4

Oven temperature
180°C, 350°F, Gas 4

Walnuts can be roasted in
the microwave. To roast in
the microwave, place the
walnuts on a glass or
ceramic microwave-safe
dish and cook, stirring every 2
minutes, on HIGH (100%) for
4-5 minutes or until nuts are
roasted. Do not use a
microwave-safe plastic
container for roasting nuts as
the oil that comes out of the
nuts during roasting can
cause the container to
bubble or melt.

CURRIED CHICKEN SALAD

1 cup/250 mL/8 fl oz dry white wine
1 cup/250 mL/8 fl oz water
1 small onion, chopped
freshly ground black pepper
6 chicken pieces, skin removed
$^1/_2$ green pepper, diced
$^1/_2$ red pepper, diced
2 stalks celery, chopped
1 mango, sliced

CURRIED DRESSING
2 teaspoons vegetable oil
1 onion, sliced
1 teaspoon curry powder
$^3/_4$ cup/155 g/5 oz natural yogurt
1 tablespoon chopped mango chutney

1 Place wine, water, onion and black pepper to taste in a saucepan and bring to simmering. Add chicken and poach for 30-35 minutes or until chicken is tender. Remove chicken from poaching liquid and chill. Strain liquid and refrigerate or freeze for using as stock in another recipe.

2 To make dressing, heat oil in a frying pan, add onion and curry powder and cook, stirring, for 4-5 minutes or until onion is soft. Transfer to a small bowl, add yogurt and mango chutney and mix to combine.

3 Place cold chicken, red and green pepper and celery in a bowl. Spoon over dressing and toss gently to coat chicken pieces. Cover and chill until ready to serve. Just prior to serving, top salad with mango slices.

Serves 6

If fresh mangoes are unavailable this salad can be made using drained canned mangoes or a segmented orange instead.

CHICKEN AND VEGETABLE SALAD

500 g/1 lb broccoli, broken into florets
2 carrots, sliced diagonally
1 cooked chicken, skin removed and flesh cut into bite-sized pieces
1 avocado, stoned, peeled and chopped

GINGER DRESSING
1 tablespoon soy sauce
1 teaspoon grated fresh ginger
$^1/_2$ teaspoon sesame oil
$^1/_4$ cup/60 mL/2 fl oz French dressing
freshly ground black pepper

1 Boil or microwave broccoli and carrots until just tender. Drain, refresh under cold running water, drain again and set aside to cool completely.

2 Place broccoli, carrots, chicken and avocado in a salad bowl.

3 To make dressing, place soy sauce, ginger, oil, French dressing and black pepper to taste in a screwtop jar and shake well to combine. Spoon dressing over salad and toss to combine.

Serves 6

Sesame oil is a strong-flavoured oil extracted from sesame seeds that adds a nutty flavour to food. It is of Asian origin and is available from Asian food stores and some supermarkets. Care should be taken when using sesame oil, as a little adds a lot of taste.

Chicken and Melon Salad

CHICKEN AND MELON SALAD

$^1/_4$ small watermelon
$^1/_2$ honeydew melon
$^1/_2$ rockmelon (cantaloupe)
1 x 1.5 kg/3 lb smoked chicken, skin
removed and flesh cut into strips
4 tablespoons chopped fresh coriander
freshly ground black pepper
$^1/_4$ cup/60 mL/2 fl oz French dressing

1   Remove skin and seeds from watermelon, honeydew melon and rockmelon (cantaloupe) and cut flesh into batons.

2   Place watermelon, honeydew melon, rockmelon (cantaloupe) and chicken in a bowl and toss to combine.

3   Sprinkle salad with coriander, season to taste with black pepper and spoon over French dressing. Toss to combine.

Serves 4

This salad is delicious made with any combination of melons – so choose your favourite ones or those that are available.

SNACKS

Tacos, burgers and open sandwiches are
all wonderful snack foods or light meals. Homemade, using
chicken, they make healthy and nutritious alternatives
to commercial fast foods.

Chicken Tacos

CHICKEN TACOS

1 tablespoon vegetable oil
1 large onion, finely chopped
2 cloves garlic, crushed
500 g/1 lb chicken mince
2 tablespoons (30 g/1 oz packet)
taco seasoning mix
$^1/_2$ cup/125 mL/4 fl oz water
3 tablespoons taco sauce
8 taco shells, warmed
60 g/2 oz grated tasty cheese
(mature Cheddar)

1   Heat oil in a large frying pan and cook onion and garlic over a medium heat for 3-4 minutes or until onion is soft. Add chicken and cook, stirring, for 5-6 minutes or until chicken changes colour. Stir in taco seasoning mix, water and taco sauce, bring to simmering and simmer for 4-5 minutes.

2   Divide chicken mixture between taco shells, top with grated cheese and serve with extra taco sauce if desired.

Serves 4

Taco shells are a great store-cupboard item. This recipe could also be made using leftover roast chicken. If using cooked chicken, remove skin, and mince or finely chop chicken. Cook as in recipe but only cook chicken for 2-3 minutes.

BACON AND CHICKEN LIVER KEBABS

500 g/1 lb chicken livers, trimmed
$^3/_4$ cup/185 mL/6 fl oz brandy
2 cloves garlic, crushed
220 g/7 oz rashers bacon, rinds removed

1   Place chicken livers, brandy and garlic in a bowl and toss to combine. Cover and set aside to marinate for 1 hour. Drain chicken livers. Cut bacon rashers in half and wrap around each liver.

2   Thread three bacon-wrapped livers onto lightly oiled bamboo skewers and cook under a preheated grill for 2 minutes each side or until bacon is crisp and livers are cooked.

Serves 4

When cooking chicken livers, take care not to overcook them or they will be dry and tough. Perfectly cooked chicken liver should still be slightly pink inside.

Healthy Chicken Burgers

HEALTHY CHICKEN BURGERS

4 thick slices tomato
4 hamburger buns, split and toasted
8 slices cucumber
4 lettuce leaves
30 g/1 oz alfalfa sprouts

CHICKEN PATTIES
500 g/1 lb chicken mince
1 egg, lightly beaten
**$^1/_2$ cup/30 g/1 oz bread crumbs,
made from stale bread**
2 teaspoons Worcestershire sauce
30 g/1 oz butter

1 To make patties, place chicken mince, egg, bread crumbs and Worcestershire sauce in a bowl and mix to combine. Shape mixture into eight patties, place on a plate, cover and refrigerate for 20-30 minutes.

2 Melt butter in a large frying pan and cook patties, pressing down with a spatula, for 3-4 minutes each side or until cooked. Remove patties from pan and drain on absorbent kitchen paper.

3 To assemble burgers, place a tomato slice on the bottom half of each bun, top with 2 patties, 2 cucumber slices, a lettuce leaf, a few alfalfa sprouts and top half of bun. Serve immediately.

Serves 4

A burger made with lots of healthy salad ingredients and a patty of lean chicken is just the right snack or light meal for weekend fare. If you cannot purchase chicken mince, you can make your own using 500 g/ 1 lb boneless chicken breast fillets. Remove skin from fillets before mincing.

CHICKEN AND PEPPER TORTILLAS

3 tablespoons tomato paste (purée)
125 g/4 oz grated tasty cheese
(mature Cheddar)
250 g/8 oz chopped cooked chicken
1/2 green pepper, chopped
1 fresh red chilli, seeds removed
and chopped

TORTILLAS
1 1/2 cups/250 g/8 oz polenta (corn meal)
1 1/2 cups/185 g/12 oz flour
pinch salt
75 g/2 1/2 oz butter, chopped
3/4 cup/185 mL/6 fl oz warm water

1   To make Tortillas, place polenta (corn meal), flour, salt and butter in a food processor and process until mixture resembles fine bread crumbs. With machine running, slowly add water to form a dough. Turn dough onto a lightly floured surface and knead for 2 minutes.

2   Roll out dough and, using a 10 cm/4 in round cutter, cut out eight circles. Place rounds on a lightly greased baking tray and bake for 10 minutes.

3   Spread each tortilla with tomato paste (purée), sprinkle with cheese, chicken, green pepper and chilli and bake for 10 minutes.

Makes 8 tortillas

Oven temperature
180°C, 350°F, Gas 4

In Mexico, thin pancakes made of corn meal are called tortillas, while in Spain a tortilla is a flat omelette.

Chicken and Pepper Tortillas

BUTTERMILK MUFFINS WITH TURKEY

Oven temperature
180°C, 350°F, Gas 4

Buttermilk is a cultured dairy product that has the same food value as skim milk. It is a useful low-fat ingredient that is sometimes used in baked goods.

60 g/2 oz butter
250 g/8 oz sliced smoked turkey
$^1/_2$ cup/155 g/5 oz guava, apple
or redcurrant jelly

BUTTERMILK MUFFINS
125 g/4 oz butter
$^1/_2$ cup/100 g/3$^1/_2$ oz caster sugar
2 eggs
60 g/2 oz sultanas, chopped
60 g/2 oz walnuts, chopped
1 teaspoon bicarbonate of soda
1 cup/250 mL/8 fl oz buttermilk or milk
2 cups/250 g/8 oz flour, sifted

1   To make muffins, place butter and sugar in a bowl and beat until creamy. Add eggs, one at a time, beating well after each addition. Stir in sultanas and walnuts. Dissolve bicarbonate of soda in buttermilk or milk. Fold flour and milk mixture, alternately, into creamed mixture.

2   Spoon batter into greased muffin pans and cook for 12 minutes or until golden and cooked when tested with a skewer. Turn on a wire rack to cool.

3   Split muffins, spread lightly with butter. Top bottom half with turkey slices, guava jelly and top of muffin.

Makes 15 muffins

Buttermilk Muffins with Turkey

54

Grilled Avocado Sandwiches

GRILLED AVOCADO SANDWICHES

4 thick slices brown bread
60 g/2 oz cream cheese, softened
4 tablespoons mayonnaise
250 g/8 oz cooked chicken, sliced
4 slices tasty cheese (mature Cheddar)
1 avocado, stoned, peeled and sliced
1 tablespoon snipped fresh chives

1 Spread each slice of bread with cream cheese, then mayonnaise. Top with chicken and a cheese slice. Cook under a preheated grill for 2-3 minutes or until cheese melts.

2 Top with avocado slices, sprinkle with chives and serve immediately.

Serves 4

TURKEY TRIANGLES

155 g/5 oz prepared puff pastry

TURKEY FILLING
**4 slices smoked turkey, chopped
2 tablespoons sour cream
1 tablespoon cranberry sauce
2 teaspoons snipped fresh chives
freshly ground black pepper**

Oven temperature
220°C, 425°F, Gas 7

It is worth making double the quantity of this recipe so that you can freeze the triangles to have on hand for snacks and light meals. Freeze triangles in an airtight freezerproof container or sealed freezer bag. Reheat in oven at 180°C/350°F/Gas 4 for 10-15 minutes or until heated.

1   Roll out pastry to 3 mm/^{1}/8 in thickness and cut into four 12 cm/5 in squares.

2   To make filling, place turkey, sour cream, cranberry sauce, chives and black pepper to taste in a small bowl and mix to combine. Place a spoonful of filling in the centre of each pastry square. Fold opposite pastry corners together to form a triangle. Brush edges with a little water and press together, using a fork to seal and make a decorative edge. Place on a greased baking tray and bake for 15 minutes or until pastry is puffed and golden.

Makes 4 triangles

TURKEY AND STILTON SANDWICHES

**1 French bread stick, cut into
12 thick slices
2 tablespoons Dijon mustard
12 slices smoked turkey
200 g/6^1/$_2$ oz Stilton cheese, crumbled
30 g/1 oz watercress, broken into sprigs**

Spread each slice of bread with mustard. Top with turkey and cheese and garnish with watercress. Serve immediately.

Serves 6

Every country seems to have its own favourite blue cheese. Stilton is the blue cheese of Britain. For these sandwiches you can choose your favourite blue cheese. If you do not like blue cheese you might like to use Brie, Camembert or a cream cheese instead.

QUICK MEALS

*Chicken is ideal for those times when a substantial meal
is required but time is short. This chapter provides recipes to fit
that bill perfectly. It is filled with wonderful ideas for quick
family meals and impromptu entertaining.*

Chicken Waldorf Loaf

CHICKEN WALDORF LOAF

1 cottage loaf
1 Granny Smith apple, finely chopped
60 g/2 oz walnuts, chopped
3 spring onions, finely chopped
2 tablespoons chopped fresh parsley
¹/₂ cup/125 g/4 oz mayonnaise
freshly ground black pepper
10 spinach leaves, stalks removed
and discarded
3 boneless chicken breast fillets,
cooked and sliced
4 tomatoes, sliced

1   Cut top off the loaf and scoop out middle, so that only the crust remains as a large bread case. Reserve top of loaf. The crumbs from the centre will not be used in this recipe, but can be made into bread crumbs.

2   Place apple, walnuts, spring onions, parsley, mayonnaise and black pepper to taste in a bowl and mix to combine. Place a layer of spinach leaves in base of bread case, top with a layer of chicken, a layer of apple mixture and finally a layer of tomato slices. Repeat layers, ending with a layer of spinach, until all ingredients are used and loaf is filled. Replace top and wrap loaf in aluminium foil. Place a board on top of loaf, weight down and refrigerate overnight. Serve cut into wedges.

Serves 8

A perfect picnic dish – delicate chicken breasts are combined with Waldorf salad ingredients, placed in a bread case, wrapped in aluminium foil and refrigerated overnight. All you have to do in the morning is pack the picnic basket and you are ready to go.

CRUSTY PARMESAN DRUMSTICKS

3 tablespoons Dijon mustard
4 tablespoons vegetable oil
4 spring onions, finely chopped
30 g/1 oz grated fresh Parmesan cheese
freshly ground black pepper
8 chicken drumsticks
¹/₂ cup/30 g/1 oz bread crumbs, made
from stale bread
60 g/2 oz butter, melted

1   Place mustard, oil, spring onions, Parmesan cheese and black pepper to taste in a bowl and mix to combine.

2   Brush each drumstick with mustard mixture, then roll in bread crumbs and place in a lightly greased baking dish. Pour butter over drumsticks and bake for 30 minutes or until drumsticks are cooked.

Serves 4

Oven temperature
180°C, 350°F, Gas 4

Crispy on the outside and moist inside, these drumsticks are a popular family meal. Serve with mashed potatoes and a green salad for one of the easiest meals you will ever make.

TURKEY CROQUETTES

90 g/3 oz butter
1^1/$_3$ cups/170 g/5^1/$_2$ oz flour
1 cup/250 mL/8 fl oz hot milk
125 g/4 oz ricotta cheese
250 g/8 oz cooked turkey, chopped
^{1}/$_2$ cup/60 g/2 oz grated tasty cheese
(mature Cheddar)
2 tablespoons chopped fresh parsley
1 cup/125 g/4 oz dried bread crumbs
1 egg, lightly beaten
oil for deep frying

Croquettes are a great way to use any leftover poultry or meat. In this recipe turkey has been used, but you could use leftover chicken, lamb or beef. Canned tuna or salmon are delicious alternatives. If using canned food, drain off any liquid first.

Turkey Croquettes

Serves 4

1 Melt butter in a saucepan, stir in ^{1}/$_3$ cup/45 g/1^1/$_2$ oz flour and cook, stirring, for 30 seconds. Whisk in milk and cook, stirring, over a medium heat for 4-5 minutes or until mixture thickens. Remove pan from heat and stir in ricotta cheese, turkey, tasty cheese (mature Cheddar) and parsley. Mix well to combine and refrigerate until completely cold.

2 Place bread crumbs and remaining flour on separate plates and set aside. Shape turkey mixture into croquette shapes, roll each croquette in flour, then dip in egg and roll in bread crumbs. Place on a plate lined with plastic food wrap, cover and chill for 15 minutes.

3 Heat oil in a large saucepan until hot and cook croquettes for 3-4 minutes or until golden.

Chicken Sauté

CHICKEN SAUTE

2 tablespoons vegetable oil
1 onion, sliced
1 green pepper, cut into strips
1 red pepper, cut into strips
1 zucchini (courgette), sliced
1$^1/_2$ cups/375 mL/12 fl oz tomato purée
1 tablespoon chopped fresh basil
1 tablespoon chopped fresh parsley
1 teaspoon chopped fresh thyme or
$^1/_2$ teaspoon dried thyme
500 g/1 lb boneless chicken breast
fillets, cut into strips
freshly ground black pepper

1   Heat oil in a large frying pan and cook onion over a medium heat for 5 minutes or until soft. Add green and red pepper, zucchini (courgette) and tomato purée and bring to the boil, then reduce heat and simmer for 10 minutes.

2   Stir in basil, parsley, thyme and chicken and cook for 10 minutes or until chicken is cooked. Season to taste with black pepper.

Serves 4

A medley of summer vegetables and chicken makes a quick and easy sauté that is delicious served with boiled noodles tossed in butter and finely chopped fresh parsley.

61

Chicken with Curry Sauce

CHICKEN WITH CURRY SAUCE

Spatchcocking a bird means to split and flatten it. The easiest way to cut the bird is to use a pair of poultry shears. First cut off the wing tips then cut the bird along each side of the backbone to remove it. Now place the bird breast side up and using the heel of your hand push down sharply to flatten the bird and break the breastbone. To ensure that the bird holds its shape during cooking, thread two skewers through it. One skewer is threaded through the legs, avoiding the bones, and the other through the wings and breast.

60 g/2 oz butter
4 boneless chicken breast fillets,
skin removed
1 onion, chopped
1 clove garlic, crushed
1 tablespoon curry powder
$^1/_2$ teaspoon ground cumin
$^1/_2$ teaspoon ground coriander
1 tablespoon honey
1 tablespoon fresh lemon juice
$^1/_3$ cup/90 mL/3 fl oz red wine
$^3/_4$ cup/185 mL/6 fl oz cream (double)
2 tablespoons mayonnaise
2 tablespoons chopped fresh coriander

Serves 4

1   Melt butter in a large frying pan and cook chicken over a medium heat for 3-4 minutes each side or until cooked. Remove chicken from pan, set aside and keep warm.

2   Add onion and garlic to pan and cook for 3-4 minutes or until onion is soft. Stir in curry powder, cumin and coriander, and cook for 2 minutes longer.

3   Stir in honey, lemon juice and wine, and cook for 2 minutes, then stir in cream and mayonnaise, and simmer for 2 minutes longer. Spoon sauce over chicken, sprinkle with coriander and serve immediately.

GRILLED HONEY CHICKEN

1 x 1.5 kg/3 lb chicken

HONEY GLAZE
3 tablespoons honey
2 teaspoons ground ginger
3 tablespoons Worcestershire sauce
2 tablespoons soy sauce
2 cloves garlic, crushed

1   Preheat grill to medium. Spatchcock chicken (see hint opposite) and place on a baking tray.

2   To make glaze, place honey, ginger, Worcestershire sauce, soy sauce and garlic in a small saucepan and bring to the boil over a medium heat. Brush glaze over chicken and cook under grill for 10-15 minutes each side or until chicken is cooked.

Grilled Honey Chicken

Serves 4

Chicken Stroganoff

CHICKEN STROGANOFF

90 g/2 oz butter
500 g/1 lb boneless chicken breast
fillets, cut into strips
155 g/5 oz button mushrooms, halved
$^1/_2$ cup/125 mL/4 fl oz dry white wine
1 cup/250 mL/8 fl oz cream (double)
2 tablespoons tomato paste (purée)
$^1/_2$ teaspoon ground nutmeg
1 spring onion, finely chopped

1 Melt 60 g/2 oz butter in a large frying pan and cook chicken, stirring, over a medium heat for 2-3 minutes or until chicken just changes colour. Remove chicken from pan and set aside.

2 Melt remaining butter in pan and cook mushrooms for 2-3 minutes, then stir in wine, cream, tomato paste (purée) and nutmeg. Cook, stirring, over a high heat for 5 minutes or until sauce reduces and thickens slightly.

3 Add chicken to mushroom mixture and cook, stirring, over a medium heat, for 3-4 minutes or until chicken is cooked. Stir in spring onion and serve immediately.

Serves 4

Serve Chicken Stroganoff on a bed of boiled white or brown rice accompanied by a seasonal green vegetable – asparagus or green beans are delicious.

CHICKEN CASSEROLE

2 tablespoons vegetable oil
4 boneless chicken breast fillets,
cut into strips
1 turnip, cut into strips
2 onions, chopped
440 g/14 oz canned pimentos, drained
and cut into strips
1 cup/250 mL/8 fl oz dry white wine
440 g/14 oz canned tomatoes,
undrained and mashed
3 tablespoons chopped fresh basil

1   Heat oil in a large frying pan and cook chicken over a medium heat, stirring, for 2-3 minutes or until chicken just changes colour. Remove chicken from pan and set aside.

2   Add turnip, onions and pimentos to frying pan and cook for 3-4 minutes. Stir in wine and tomatoes and bring to the boil over a medium heat, stirring, then reduce heat and simmer, uncovered, for 10 minutes or until turnip is tender. Return chicken to pan and cook for 3-4 minutes longer or until chicken is cooked. Stir in basil and serve immediately.

Chicken Casserole

Serves 4

All this easy chicken dish needs to make a complete meal is hot garlic bread or crusty bread rolls and a salad of mixed lettuce and herbs.

65

BASIL CHICKEN

1 tablespoon olive oil
4 boneless chicken breast fillets, cut into strips
2 leeks, white part only, sliced
125 g/4 oz button mushrooms, sliced
6 sun-dried tomatoes, drained and sliced
2 tablespoons red wine vinegar
3 tablespoons lime or lemon juice
1 small red chilli, seeded and chopped
1 tablespoon chopped fresh basil
1 tablespoon chopped fresh parsley

1 Heat oil in a large frying pan over a medium heat, add chicken and stir-fry for 5 minutes or until chicken is just cooked. Remove chicken from pan, set aside and keep warm.

2 Add leeks, mushrooms, sun-dried tomatoes, vinegar, lime or lemon juice, chilli, basil and parsley to pan and cook, stirring, for 3 minutes.

3 Return chicken to pan and cook, stirring, for 2-3 minutes longer.

Serves 4

This dish is delicious served with boiled noodles or pasta of your choice and a tossed green salad.

HONEY CHICKEN KEBABS

15 g/¹/₂ oz butter
1 tablespoon honey
3 tablespoons lemon juice
2 teaspoons apricot jam
2 teaspoons finely grated lemon rind
freshly ground black pepper
4 boneless chicken breast fillets, cut into
2 cm/³/₄ in cubes
2 red peppers, cut into 2 cm/³/₄ in cubes

YOGURT SAUCE
¹/₂ cup/100 g/3¹/₂ oz natural yogurt
1 tablespoon lemon juice
1 clove garlic, crushed
¹/₄ teaspoon ground coriander
¹/₄ teaspoon ground cumin

Serves 4

1 Melt butter in a large frying pan over a medium heat, add honey, lemon juice, apricot jam, lemon rind and black pepper to taste and cook, stirring, for 1-2 minutes or until honey and jam are melted and mixture is combined.

2 Thread chicken and red pepper cubes, alternately, onto eight lightly oiled bamboo skewers. Place skewers in pan and cook, turning frequently, for 7-10 minutes or until chicken is cooked through.

3 To make sauce, place yogurt, lemon juice, garlic, coriander, cumin and black pepper to taste in bowl and mix to combine.

4 To serve, place kebabs on a bed of rice, spoon over sauce and serve immediately.

For something different you might like to serve these kebabs on a bed of yellow rice. To achieve the yellow colour add a little ground turmeric to the water before cooking.

Below: Peppered Chicken
Right: Indonesian Chicken

PEPPERED CHICKEN

2 tablespoons cracked black peppercorns
8 boneless chicken breast fillets
60 g/2 oz butter
$^1/_2$ cup/125 mL/4 fl oz dry sherry
1 cup/250 mL/8 fl oz cream (double)

A quick and delicious dish
that is ideal for impromptu
entertaining. For a complete
meal serve with crusty bread
or rolls, steamed green beans
and cherry tomatoes.

1   Sprinkle peppercorns over chicken
breasts and lightly pound to slightly
flatten the chicken.

2   Melt butter in a large frying pan over a
medium heat, add chicken to pan and
cook for 4-5 minutes each side or until
chicken is cooked through. Remove
chicken from pan, set aside and keep
warm.

3   Add sherry and cream to pan, bring to
the boil, reduce heat and simmer for 10-
15 minutes or until sauce is reduced by
half. Spoon sauce over chicken and serve.

Serves 4

Indonesian Chicken

3 tablespoons vegetable oil
4 boneless chicken breast fillets, cut into
2 cm/^{3}/4 in cubes
250 g/8 oz green beans, cut into 2.5 cm/
1 in pieces
^{1}/4 cup/60 mL/2 fl oz lemon juice
2 tablespoons soy sauce
1 tablespoon brown sugar
2 teaspoons ground turmeric
^{1}/2 cup/125 mL/4 fl oz water

1   Heat oil in a wok or frying pan, add chicken and stir-fry for 3-4 minutes or until chicken browns. Remove chicken from pan and set aside.

2   Add beans to pan and stir-fry for 2 minutes. Stir in lemon juice, soy sauce, sugar, turmeric and water, bring to the boil and simmer for 3-5 minutes or until beans are tender and sauce reduces and thickens slightly. Return chicken to pan and cook for 2-3 minutes longer or until chicken is cooked through.

Serves 4

For successful stir-frying, heat your wok until very hot, then add the oil, swirl the wok to coat the surface, continue to heat until the oil is almost smoking before adding the food. Following this procedure will ensure that the food does not stick to wok. The exception to this is when the first ingredients to be added to the wok are garlic, spring onions, ginger or chillies. Add these ingredients immediately after adding the oil or they will burn.

CHICKEN WITH PEANUTS

500 g/1 lb chicken breast fillets, cut into
2.5 cm/1 in cubes
$^1/_3$ cup/90 mL/3 fl oz dry white wine
1 teaspoon grated fresh ginger
1 clove garlic, crushed
1 tablespoon vegetable oil
1 cup/250 mL/8 fl oz chicken stock
$^1/_3$ cup/90 g/3 oz crunchy peanut butter
2 spring onions, cut into thin strips
1 red chilli, sliced

1   Place chicken, wine, ginger and garlic in a bowl and mix to combine. Cover and set aside to marinate for 30 minutes. Drain and reserve marinade.

2   Heat oil in a wok or large frying pan, add chicken and stir-fry for 7-10 minutes or until chicken is almost cooked. Add reserved marinade, stock and peanut butter to pan and bring to the boil. Reduce heat and simmer for 5 minutes or until sauce reduces and thickens slightly. Add spring onions and chilli and cook for 1 minute longer. Serve immediately.

For a complete meal, serve this easy chicken dish with boiled white or brown rice and steamed snow peas (mangetout) or cabbage.

Serves 4

70

STIR-FRY CHICKEN WITH CASHEWS

2 tablespoons vegetable oil
1 red onion, cut into wedges, separated
1 carrot, sliced diagonally
1 clove garlic, crushed
1 teaspoon grated fresh ginger
375 g/12 oz boneless chicken breast
fillets, cut into strips
1 head broccoli, cut into florets
60 g/2 oz unsalted cashews
$^1/_2$ cup/125 mL/4 fl oz chicken stock
2 teaspoons cornflour
2 teaspoons soy sauce
1 tablespoon dry sherry
$^1/_4$ teaspoon sesame oil
3 spring onions, sliced diagonally

1 Heat 1 tablespoon oil in a wok or large frying pan, add onion and carrot and stir-fry for 5 minutes. Add garlic and ginger and cook for 1 minute longer. Remove vegetable mixture from pan and set aside.

2 Add chicken to pan and stir-fry for 2-3 minutes or until lightly browned. Remove and set aside.

3 Heat remaining oil in pan, add broccoli and cashews and stir-fry until broccoli just changes colour and cashews are golden.

4 Combine stock, cornflour, soy sauce, sherry and sesame oil. Return vegetable mixture and chicken to pan, add cornflour mixture and cook, stirring constantly, for 3-4 minutes or until sauce boils and thickens. Stir in spring onions and serve immediately.

Serves 4

Stir-frying is one of the most popular methods of Chinese cooking. A wok is best for stir-frying but a large frying pan can be used if you do not have a wok. As stir-frying is so quick it is important that you have all your ingredients prepared before you start cooking.

LEFTOVERS

*Turkey is a must for Christmas and
Thanksgiving. But what do you do with the leftovers?
This selection of easy ideas will have you cooking turkey
often, just so you can use the leftovers.*

Turkey Tetrazzini

Turkey Creole

Turkey Noodle Bake

Turkey Hash

Chicken Waldorf
Millefeuille

Quick Turkey Divan

Turkey and Feta Salad

Turkey Tetrazzini

Turkey Tetrazzini

90 g/3 oz plain tagliatelle
90 g/3 oz tomato tagliatelle
90 g/3 oz spinach tagliatelle
60 g/2 oz butter
4 rashers bacon, chopped
1 onion, chopped
125 g/4 oz mushrooms, sliced
^{1}/3 cup/45 g/1^1/2 oz flour
1^3/4 cups/440 mL/14 fl oz chicken stock
^{3}/4 cup/185 mL/6 fl oz cream (double)
2 tablespoons dry sherry
375 g/12 oz cooked turkey, cubed
pinch ground nutmeg
freshly ground black pepper
30 g/1 oz grated Parmesan cheese

1   Cook plain, tomato and spinach tagliatelle together in a large saucepan of boiling water following packet instructions. Drain, set aside and keep warm.

2   Melt butter in a saucepan and cook bacon and onion, stirring, over a medium heat for 4-5 minutes or until onion is soft. Add mushrooms and cook, stirring, for 5 minutes longer or until mushrooms are soft.

3   Stir in flour, then gradually stir in stock and bring to the boil. Reduce heat and simmer, stirring, for 4-5 minutes or until sauce thickens. Remove pan from heat and stir in cream, sherry, turkey, nutmeg, black pepper to taste and tagliatelle.

4   Spoon mixture into an ovenproof dish, sprinkle with Parmesan cheese and bake for 30 minutes or until top is golden.

Serves 4

Oven temperature
180°C, 350°F, Gas 4

When storing leftover turkey, remove the stuffing from the carcass and place in a separate bowl. Cover and refrigerate turkey and stuffing separately.

Turkey Creole

15 g/^{1}/2 oz butter
1 clove garlic, crushed
1 onion, chopped
1 tablespoon flour
1 teaspoon chilli powder
^{1}/2 cup/125 mL/4 fl oz tomato juice
^{1}/2 cup/125 mL/4 fl oz chicken stock
375 g/12 oz cooked turkey, chopped
125 g/4 oz button mushrooms, sliced
freshly ground black pepper

1   Heat butter in a saucepan and cook garlic and onion over a medium heat for 3-4 minutes or until onion is soft. Stir in flour and chilli powder and cook, stirring, for 1 minute.

2   Stir in tomato juice and stock. Bring to the boil, stirring, over a medium heat, then reduce heat and simmer, stirring, until sauce thickens. Add turkey and mushrooms, season to taste with black pepper, bring to the boil, then reduce heat and simmer for 5 minutes.

Serves 4

Served on a bed of boiled rice, this makes a complete meal that is just right for the day after a feast.

TURKEY NOODLE BAKE

Oven temperature
180°C, 350°F, Gas 4

Remember cooked poultry is best used the next day and should always be used within two days of cooking.

375 g/12 oz egg noodles, cooked
250 g/8 oz cooked turkey, chopped
60 g/2 oz grated tasty cheese
(mature Cheddar)
2 stalks celery, chopped
2 cups/500 mL/16 fl oz milk
2 eggs
1 teaspoon curry powder
freshly ground black pepper
1/2 cup/30 g/1 oz bread crumbs,
made from stale bread
15 g/1 oz butter

1 Place one-third of noodles in base of a lightly greased ovenproof dish. Top with one-third each of turkey, cheese and celery. Repeat layers until all ingredients are used.

2 Place milk, eggs, curry powder and black pepper to taste in a bowl and whisk to combine. Carefully pour milk mixture over ingredients in dish, sprinkle with bread crumbs and dot with butter. Bake for 40 minutes or until firm.

Serves 6

TURKEY HASH

This tasty dish uses those foods that are most often leftover and turns them into something special. If you do not have leftover gravy, use cream of mushroom soup instead.

375 g/12 oz cooked turkey, chopped
2 potatoes, cooked and diced
1 cup/250 mL/8 fl oz leftover
turkey gravy
2 spring onions, chopped
freshly ground black pepper
4 slices wholegrain bread, toasted
and lightly buttered
2 tablespoons chopped fresh parsley

1 Place turkey, potatoes, gravy, spring onions and black pepper to taste in a saucepan and bring to the boil, stirring, over a medium heat.

2 Spoon turkey mixture over hot toast, sprinkle with parsley and serve immediately.

Serves 4

Turkey Noodle Bake, Turkey Creole, Quick
Turkey Divan, Turkey Hash

CHICKEN WALDORF MILLEFEUILLE

Oven temperature
220°C, 425°F, Gas 7

200 g/6¹/₂ oz prepared puff pastry,
thawed
1 egg, lightly beaten
315 g/10 oz cooked chopped chicken
1 green apple, peeled, cored and
thinly sliced
2 stalks celery, sliced
2 tablespoons sultanas
3 tablespoons pecans, roughly chopped

BRANDY MAYONNAISE
3 tablespoons mayonnaise
¹/₂ cup/125 mL/4 fl oz cream (double)
1 tablespoon brandy
pinch ground turmeric
¹/₂ teaspoon Dijon mustard
2 teaspoons chopped capers
2 teaspoons snipped fresh chives

1   Roll pastry out to 3 mm/¹/₈ in
thickness and cut out six rectangles each
8 x 12 cm/3¹/₄ x 5 in. Place pastry
rectangles on greased baking trays, brush
with egg and bake for 10-12 minutes or
until golden.

2   Place chicken, apple, celery, sultanas
and pecans in a bowl and mix to
combine.

3   To make mayonnaise, place
mayonnaise, cream, brandy, turmeric,
mustard, capers and chives in a bowl and
mix to combine. Spoon mayonnaise over
chicken mixture and toss to coat.

4   To assemble, slit pastry rectangles
horizontally. Place a pastry rectangle on
four individual serving plates, top with
half the chicken mixture, then another
pastry layer. Repeat with remaining
chicken mixture and pastry layers.
Refrigerate until required.

Serves 4

Chicken Waldorf Millefeuille

Quick Turkey Divan

4 slices bread, toasted and
lightly buttered
8 slices cooked turkey
375 g/12 oz canned asparagus
spears, drained
1 cup/250 mL/8 fl oz cream of
asparagus soup
1 cup/250 mL/8 fl oz evaporated milk
freshly ground black pepper
3 tablespoons grated fresh Parmesan
cheese

1 Place toast in base of a lightly greased, shallow ovenproof dish. Top with turkey slices and asparagus spears.

2 Place soup, milk and black pepper to taste in a bowl and mix to combine. Carefully pour soup mixture over ingredients in dish, sprinkle with Parmesan cheese and bake for 20-25 minutes or until top is golden and mixture bubbling.

Serves 4

Oven temperature
200°C, 400°F, Gas 6

Turkey and Feta Salad

500 g/1 lb cooked turkey, cut into
bite-sized pieces
2 stalks celery, chopped
1 cucumber, peeled, seeded and chopped
12 black olives, pitted
250 g/8 oz feta cheese
1 bunch curly endive
1 small bunch watercress

BASIL VINAIGRETTE
1 clove garlic, crushed
4 tablespoons chopped fresh basil
2 tablespoons grain mustard
freshly ground black pepper
$^1/_4$ cup/60 mL/2 fl oz fresh lemon juice
$^1/_4$ cup/60 mL/2 fl oz red wine vinegar
$^1/_4$ cup/60 mL/2 fl oz vegetable oil
$^1/_4$ cup/60 mL/2 fl oz olive oil

1 To make vinaigrette, place garlic, basil, mustard, black pepper to taste, lemon juice, vinegar and vegetable and olive oils in a screwtop jar and shake well to combine.

2 Place turkey, celery, cucumber, olives and feta cheese in a bowl. Pour over vinaigrette and toss to combine.

3 Arrange endive leaves on four individual plates, top with salad and garnish with watercress. Serve immediately.

Serves 6 as a light meal

Serve this delicious one-dish salad with crusty rolls or bread for a complete meal.

FRENCH ROAST CHICKEN

1 x 1.5 kg/3 lb chicken
1 cup/250 mL/8 fl oz dry white wine
1 cup/250 mL/8 fl oz chicken stock
30 g/1 oz butter

CHEESE STUFFING
90 g/3 oz ricotta cheese
2 tablespoons chopped fresh parsley
2 teaspoons chopped fresh tarragon or
$^1/_2$ teaspoon dried tarragon leaves
4 spring onions, finely chopped
30 g/1 oz butter, softened
freshly ground black pepper

HERB STUFFING
60 g/2 oz butter
1 small onion, finely chopped
2 stalks celery, finely chopped
2 teaspoons chopped fresh tarragon or
$^1/_2$ teaspoon dried tarragon
2 tablespoons chopped fresh parsley

1 teaspoon finely grated lemon rind
2 cups/125 g/4 oz bread crumbs, made
from stale bread
freshly ground black pepper

GRAVY
$1^1/_2$ cups/375 mL/12 fl oz cooking
liquid and chicken stock
1 tablespoon cornflour
$^1/_2$ cup/125 mL/4 fl oz cream (double)
freshly ground black pepper

French Roast Chicken

1   To make Cheese Stuffing, place ricotta cheese, parsley, tarragon, spring onions, butter and black pepper to taste in a bowl and mix to combine.

2   Using your fingers, loosen skin on breast of chicken. Push Cheese Stuffing gently under skin, smoothing out evenly.

3   To make Herb Stuffing, melt butter in a saucepan and cook onion for 4-5 minutes or until soft. Place celery, tarragon, parsley, lemon rind and bread crumbs in a bowl, add onion mixture and mix to combine. Season to taste with black pepper. Spoon stuffing into cavity of chicken and secure neck end with metal or bamboo skewers.

4   Truss chicken and place breast side up on a wire rack set in a baking dish. Place wine, stock and butter in dish and bake chicken, turning and basting several times, for 1 hour or until skin is crisp and golden, and chicken is cooked. For the last 15 minutes of cooking, turn the chicken breast side up – this ensures that skin on the breast is crisp. Place chicken on a serving platter and set aside to rest in a warm place for 10 minutes before carving.

5   To make gravy, measure liquid in baking dish and, if necessary, make up to 1¹/₂ cups/375 mL/12 fl oz with chicken stock. Return liquid to baking dish. Place dish on stove (cooker) top and bring to the boil over a medium heat. Place cornflour in a small bowl and whisk in cream. Whisk a little hot liquid into the cream mixture, then stir into baking dish. Cook, stirring constantly, for 3-4 minutes or until gravy boils and thickens. Season with black pepper. Serve gravy with chicken.

Serves 4

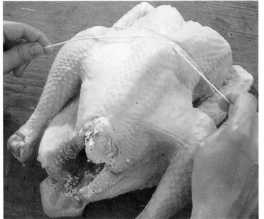

Paul E. Elson/IMAGE BANK

There should always be liquid in the base of the baking dish when roasting the chicken. If the liquid evaporates during cooking, add a little more wine or stock.

Paul E. Elson/IMAGE BANK

You might like to use blue cheese, cream cheese or Camembert in place of the ricotta cheese. If using Camembert, remove rind first.

TRUSSING A CHICKEN

Trussing a chicken helps it maintain its shape during cooking. Insert a metal skewer widthwise, just below the thigh bone, right through the body of the chicken. The ends of the skewer should be exposed either side. Place the chicken breast side down on a work surface. Take a length of string and catch in wing tips, then pass string under ends of skewer and cross over the back. Turn the chicken breast side up and tie in legs and the parson's nose.

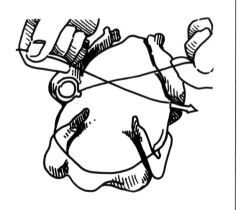

CHICKEN WITH SPINACH FILLING

Oven temperature
180°C, 350°F, Gas 4

4 chicken marylands (uncut leg and
thigh joints)
30 g/1 oz butter, melted

SPINACH FILLING
125 g/4 oz frozen spinach, thawed
1 clove garlic, crushed
125 g/4 oz ricotta or cottage cheese,
drained
2 teaspoons grated Parmesan cheese
1 teaspoon finely grated lemon rind
pinch ground nutmeg

TOMATO SAUCE
310 g/10 oz canned tomato purée
2 teaspoons Worcestershire sauce

Chicken with Spinach Filling

1   To make filling, squeeze spinach to remove excess liquid. Place spinach, garlic, ricotta or cottage cheese, Parmesan cheese, lemon rind and nutmeg in a bowl and mix to combine.

2   Using your fingers, loosen skin on chicken, starting at thigh end.

3   Push filling gently under skin down into the drumstick. Arrange chicken pieces in an ovenproof dish, brush with melted butter and bake for 35-40 minutes.

4   To make sauce, place tomato purée and Worcestershire sauce in a saucepan, bring to simmering and simmer for 3-4 minutes. Serve sauce with chicken.

Serves 4

Drumsticks can be used in place of the chicken marylands if you wish.

Frozen chicken should be completely thawed before cooking. Thaw birds in refrigerator for 24-36 hours or in microwave on DEFROST (30%) for 10-15 minutes per 500 g/1 lb of chicken. Rinse cavity of chicken under cold running water to ensure that there are no remaining ice crystals.

SPICY CHICKEN PIES

PASTRY
3 cups/375 g/12 oz flour
90 g/3 oz butter, cut into pieces
90 g/3 oz lard, cut into pieces
1/3 cup/90 mL/3 fl oz cold water
1 egg, beaten

SPICY CHICKEN FILLING
30 g/1 oz butter
60 g/2 oz button mushrooms, chopped
1 onion, chopped
2 teaspoons garam masala
1/4 cup/30 g/1 oz flour
3/4 cup/185 mL/6 fl oz chicken stock
315 g/10 oz cooked chicken, diced
60 g/2 oz sweet corn kernels
freshly ground black pepper

1 To make filling, melt butter in a saucepan and cook mushrooms, onion and garam masala over a medium heat for 3-4 minutes or until onion is soft. Stir in flour and cook for 1 minute longer. Add stock and bring to the boil, stirring constantly. Reduce heat and simmer, stirring, for 2 minutes. Remove pan from heat, stir in chicken and sweet corn, season to taste with black pepper and set aside to cool completely.

Spicy Chicken Pies

2 To make pastry, place flour, butter and lard in a food processor and process until mixture resembles fine bread crumbs. With machine running, add water and process to form a firm dough. Turn dough onto a lightly floured surface and knead until smooth.

3 Take two-thirds of the dough and cut into four portions. Roll out each portion to fit a 12.5 cm/5 in loose-based, fluted flan tin. Line flan tins with pastry, press pastry into flutes, but do not trim top edge. Cut remaining pastry into four portions and roll out each portion to make a lid for each pie.

4 Spoon cold filling into flan tins. Dampen edges of pastry in tins and cover with pastry lids. Using a flat-bladed knife, press edges together to seal and cut off excess pastry. Gather together pastry trimmings, re-roll, then cut out pastry leaves and use to decorate tops of pies. Brush tops with beaten egg.

5 Place pies on a baking tray and bake for 40-45 minutes or until pastry is golden. Remove pies from oven and set aside to cool. When cool, remove from flan tins.

Serves 4

These pies are a delicious picnic food served with a fruit chutney and a crisp salad.

'Delicious as picnic fare or in a packed lunch, you will want to keep a supply of these pies in your freezer'

PERFECT ROAST TURKEY

Oven temperature
180°C, 350°F, Gas 4

4 kg/8 lb turkey
60 g/2 oz butter, melted
1 cup/250 mL/8 fl oz chicken stock

VEAL FORCEMEAT
30 g/1 oz butter
1 onion, finely chopped
1 rasher bacon, finely chopped
250 g/8 oz lean veal mince
3 cups/185 g/6 oz bread crumbs, made
from stale bread
$^1/_2$ teaspoon finely grated lemon rind
$^1/_2$ teaspoon finely chopped fresh parsley
$^1/_2$ teaspoon dried sage
pinch ground nutmeg
1 egg, lightly beaten
freshly ground black pepper

CHESTNUT STUFFING
440 g/14 oz canned chestnut purée,
sieved
2 cooking apples, cored, peeled
and grated
3 cups/185 g/6 oz bread crumbs,
made from stale bread
1 onion, finely chopped
1 stalk celery, finely chopped
4 tablespoons finely chopped walnuts
1 tablespoon finely chopped
fresh parsley
45 g/1$^1/_2$ oz butter, melted
1 egg, lightly beaten
pinch ground nutmeg
freshly ground black pepper

Perfect Roast Turkey

84

1   To make forcemeat, melt butter in a frying pan and cook onion and bacon for 4-5 minutes or until bacon is crisp. Add veal mince, bread crumbs, lemon rind, parsley, sage, nutmeg, egg and black pepper to taste. Mix well to combine.

2   To make stuffing, place chestnut purée, apples, bread crumbs, onion, celery, walnuts, parsley, butter, egg, nutmeg and black pepper to taste in a bowl and mix to combine.

3   Remove giblets and neck from turkey. Wipe turkey inside and out and dry well. Place stuffing in body cavity and lightly fill neck end of turkey with forcemeat. Secure openings with metal or bamboo skewers. Tuck wings under body of turkey and tie legs together.

4   Place turkey on a roasting rack in a baking dish. Brush with butter, then pour chicken stock into baking dish. Bake for 3-3¹/₂ hours or until tender. Baste frequently with pan juices during cooking. Set aside in a warm place to stand for 20 minutes before carving.

Serves 10

It is safest to defrost a frozen turkey in the refrigerator for 36-48 hours. Actual defrosting time will of course depend on the size of the bird. Once defrosted, wash bird and rinse out cavity, then pat dry using absorbent kitchen paper. Make sure that there are no ice crystals left in the cavity.

'Cooks have developed many wonderful turkey dishes for special occasions with delicious stuffings and accompaniments. Try this Roast Turkey for a Christmas or Thanksgiving dinner.'

CARVING THE TURKEY

A very sharp, pointed knife with a long flexible blade is best for carving turkey. Before you start carving, remove string and skewers from bird and place breast side up on a board or platter. Use a large carving fork to hold bird steady.

1   Removing first leg: Cut skin between thigh and breast of bird. Separate leg from body by bending thigh outwards to locate hip joint. Slice down through joint to remove the leg.

2   Separating thigh from drumstick: Hold knife at an angle between thigh and drumstick bones and cut firmly through joint to separate leg.

3   Slicing drumstick: Cut a thick slice of meat and skin from each side of drumstick, keeping knife close to the bone, then cut these into smaller slices.

4   Slicing thigh: Holding thigh steady, cut into four or more pieces, depending on the size of thigh. Repeat steps 1-4 for other leg of turkey.

5   Removing wing: Slice down through corner of breast towards wing. Push wing out to show joint and cut through joint. Remove wing with piece of breast attached.

6   Carving breast: Holding breast steady, slice down through meat. When you reach incision above the wing joint, the slice will fall free.

COOKING TIMES FOR A STUFFED TURKEY

Cook turkeys at 180°C/350°F/Gas 4. If cooked in a hotter oven the outside of the bird browns and cooks before the centre.

Weight	Time
2.5-3 kg/5-6 lb	$2^1/2$-3 hours
3-4 kg/6-8 lb	3-$3^1/2$ hours
4-6 kg/8-12 lb	$3^1/2$-4 hours

CHICKEN STOCK

4 whole cloves
2 onions, halved crossways
1 chicken carcass, skin removed and
trimmed of
all visible fat
12 cups/3 litres/5 pt cold water
2 carrots, roughly chopped
4 stalks celery, roughly chopped
fresh herbs of your choice
¹/₂ teaspoon black peppercorns

1   Stick cloves into onion halves.

2   Place chicken carcass, water, carrots, celery, herbs, peppercorns and clove-studded onions in a large saucepan. Bring to the boil, reduce heat and simmer, stirring occasionally, for 2 hours.

3   Strain stock and refrigerate overnight. Skim fat from surface of stock and use as required.

Makes 8 cups/2 litres/3¹/₂ pt

The microwave is particularly good for making small quantities of stock. To make stock in the microwave, place chicken carcass remaining after a roast or raw carcass, 1 chopped onion, 1 chopped carrot, 2 stalks chopped celery, parsley and thyme in a large microwave-safe container. Add water to cover ingredients. Cook, uncovered, on HIGH (100%) for 45 minutes. Strain stock and refrigerate overnight. Skim fat from the surface and use as required.

Chicken stock is the basis of many classic dishes.
Stock will keep in the refrigerator for 3-4 days, or in the freezer
for 12 months. Freeze stock in ¹/₂ cup/125 mL/4 fl oz or
1 cup/250 mL/8 fl oz portions for easy use at a later date.

CRUSTY CHICKEN GOULASH

Oven temperature
180°C, 350°F, Gas 4

2 tablespoons vegetable oil
2 large onions, chopped
1$^1/_2$ tablespoons paprika
2 tablespoons seasoned flour
500 g/1 lb boneless chicken breast
fillets, cut into strips
1 tablespoon tomato paste (purée)
$^1/_2$ cup/125 mL/4 fl oz red wine
$^1/_2$ cup/125 mL/4 fl oz chicken stock
3 tablespoons natural yogurt

SOUR CREAM CRUST
125 g/4 oz butter, softened
300 g/9$^1/_2$ oz sour cream
1 egg
1 cup/125 g/4 oz self-raising flour, sifted
1 tablespoon chopped fresh parsley

Crusty Chicken Goulash

1   Heat 1 tablespoon oil in a large frying pan and cook onions, stirring, over a medium heat for 5-6 minutes or until golden. Remove onions from pan and set aside. Combine paprika and flour in a plastic food bag, add chicken, shake to coat with flour mixture, then shake off excess flour mixture.

2   Heat remaining oil in frying pan and cook chicken, stirring, over a medium heat for 2-3 minutes. Return onions to pan, stir in tomato paste (purée), wine and stock. Bring to the boil, stirring constantly, then reduce heat, cover and simmer for 6-7 minutes. Remove pan from heat, stir in yogurt and set aside to cool.

3   To make crust, place butter, sour cream and egg in a bowl. Stir in flour and parsley and mix well to combine.

4   To assemble, place crust mixture in an 8 cup/2 litre/3^1/2 pt lightly greased casserole dish and work mixture to cover sides and base of dish.

5   Spoon filling into crust, cover with lid of dish and bake for 35 minutes. Remove lid and bake for 10 minutes longer.

Serves 4

Serve this delicious chicken with a tossed green salad or a boiled, steamed or microwaved green vegetable such as green beans, zucchini (courgettes), snow peas (mangetout) or asparagus.

'A chicken goulash surrounded by a rich sour cream crust is just the thing for that special occasion.'

CHICKEN LIVER PATE

60 g/2 oz butter
1 onion, finely chopped
1 clove garlic, crushed
250 g/8 oz chicken livers, chopped
1-2 teaspoons curry powder
¹/₂ cup/125 mL/4 fl oz chicken stock
2 hard-boiled eggs, cut
into wedges
freshly ground black pepper
cayenne pepper
fresh bay leaves
lemon slices

1 Melt 30 g/1 oz butter in a frying pan and cook onion, garlic and chicken livers, stirring, over a medium heat for 5 minutes. Add curry powder and cook for 1 minute longer. Add stock and cook, stirring, for 5 minutes. Remove pan from heat and set aside to cool for 10 minutes.

2 Place chicken liver mixture and eggs in a food processor or blender and blend to form a smooth purée.

3 Season to taste with black and cayenne pepper. Spoon pâté into a terrine and smooth surface. Melt remaining butter and pour over pâté. Decorate with bay leaves and lemon slices. Refrigerate for several hours. Serve with biscuits or crusty bread.

MICROWAVING POULTRY

As poultry has a low fat content it does not brown naturally when cooked in the microwave, so use a baste or browning agent to add colour and flavour.

The following hints will ensure your microwaved birds are perfect:

❧ Before cooking, tuck wings under bird and tie legs together using a rubber band or string. (Rubber bands do not melt if you use them in the microwave.)

❧ Start cooking bird, breast side down and turn over halfway through cooking.

❧ If you wish your bird to have a roasted appearance and taste do not cover during cooking, as covering causes the bird to steam. Cooking a bird in a covered casserole is the ideal way to cook it if you wish to use the flesh in a soup or for chicken salad.

❧ A stuffed bird will take a little longer to cook. Add 2 minutes to the total cooking time.

❧ Cook birds elevated on a roasting rack.

❧ For larger birds, such as turkeys, you may need to shield the wings and drumsticks with aluminium foil during cooking.

❧ On completion of cooking, cover bird with aluminium foil and allow to stand for 10-15 minutes.

❧ For those working in metric measures, an easy way to calculate the cooking time of a chicken is to take its weight, remove the decimal point and cook for that many minutes each side. For example, you would cook a 1.5 kg chicken for 15 minutes each side – a total cooking time of 30 minutes. You can use a similar formula for cooking other poultry, but remember to cook turkey for the first 10 minutes on HIGH (100%) then reduce the power setting to MEDIUM-HIGH (70%).

Chicken cooks quickly in the microwave and is moist and tender.

MICROWAVE COOKING CHART

FOOD	POWER LEVEL	COOKING TIMES per 500 g/1 lb
Whole chicken	HIGH (100%)	10 minutes
Chicken pieces	HIGH (100%)	10 minutes
Turkey	HIGH (100%)	10 minutes then
	MEDIUM-HIGH (70%)	10 minutes
Quail	HIGH (100%)	8 minutes
Duck	HIGH (100%)	10 minutes
Goose	MEDIUM-HIGH (70%)	12 minutes

CHICKEN

What distinguishes a poussin from a chicken? Read on and find out the differences between the various types of birds and what to look for when buying. As part of an everyday diet, chicken is a delicious and healthy food. Most of its fat lies just under the skin, which is easily removed for low-fat cooking.

Whether it's a simple family meal or a formal dinner party, chicken has a place. In recent years its increased availability and moderate price has taken it from being a luxury food to one that can be included regularly as part of your diet.

BUYING: Whole chickens are available fresh or frozen, in a variety of sizes. When buying fresh chicken the bird should have a fresh smell; an unbroken skin with no dark patches; the breast should be plump; the tip of the breastbone soft and pliable; and there should be little moisture on the bird.

Chicken is also sold in pieces – the breast being the most tender and the leanest. Breast chicken is frequently sold as boneless breast fillets which are suitable for poaching, baking, grilling and pan cooking. The dark meat on the thighs and drumsticks is higher in fat. The uncut thigh and drumstick portion is called a chicken maryland and is popular crumbed and baked. The wings in small and average-sized birds have little meat but make great finger food when marinated and grilled, baked or barbecued. They are also often used in soups.

POUSSINS: A poussin, is a very small chicken about 6 weeks old and weighing 500 g-1 kg/1-2 lb. Usually one bird per serving is allowed. It is very tender with a delicate flavour that makes it particularly suited to roasting, pot roasting, casseroling, grilling and barbecuing.

SPRING CHICKEN: Slightly larger and a little older than a poussin, a spring chicken is about 8 weeks old and weighs about 1 kg/2 lb. One bird serves two people.

BOILING FOWLS: This is an older hen (often 18 months or older) that has stopped laying. It is tough and needs a moist method of cooking. The best way to cook a boiling fowl is to boil or stew it. The cooking time will be about 3 hours, and vegetables are added towards the end of the cooking.

TURKEY: Turkey is available in many guises. Whole birds vary greatly in size from around 2.5 kg/5 lb to as large as 13.5 kg/30 lb. Other cuts, such as turkey buffe – which is the breast with the bone in – rolled breast and fillets are also available and have the advantage of being easier to carve. Turkey hindquarters are also an economic and tasty alternative. Turkey is a nutritious low-fat food; in fact it has half the fat and a third of the cholesterol of domestic chicken.

DUCK: Duck has a similar nutrient content to chicken but has twice as much fat. To remove some of the fat during cooking, duck is often cooked on a rack set in a baking dish.

Farmed duck is available both fresh and frozen and should have creamy-white skin with a plump breast. A duck is a bird that is 2-3 months old, weighing 2-3 kg/4-6 lb, while a duckling is a smaller, younger duck of 6-8 weeks, weighing 1.5-2 kg/3-4 lb. Wild duck varies greatly in size, age and taste, and requires a moist method of cooking for best results.

QUAIL: Quail is now widely available and is a popular gourmet food. It has a delicate flesh and care should be taken during cooking to prevent it drying out. The average bird weighs 155 g/5 oz and is delicious roasted, braised, pan-cooked or made into pies and pâtés.

STORAGE: The same basic rules apply to all poultry and game birds.

A fresh bird should be removed from its wrapping and placed on a plate then covered lightly so that air can circulate around it.

If preparing the bird in advance, do not stuff it until just prior to cooking. However, the stuffing and the bird can be prepared in advance and stored separately.

To avoid the possibility of salmonella food poisoning, it is important to completely defrost a frozen bird before cooking. To defrost, leave the frozen bird in its original wrapping and place in the refrigerator for 24 hours or longer, depending on its size. Defrosting can also be done in the microwave using DEFROST (30%) and allowing 10 minutes per 500 g/1 lb.

INDEX